BE A CREATIVE EXPLORER
Creative writing, colouring-in and collage making workbook

Creative Experiences
By Corina Stupu Thomas

Published in 2019 by
KDPSelect

IBSN- 9781086321401

Created by Corina Stupu Thomas

BE A CREATIVE EXPLORER

BE A CREATIVE EXPLORER is a creative workbook, a place where you will create inspiring and engaging stories in the form of coloured images, collages, journalling entries and poems, a space where you will use your imagination to connect with the many faces of you.

Using our imagination - through storytelling in various ways - can feel overwhelming, at times exhilarating, sometimes exasperating, many times uplifting ….. but always empowering.

The good thing is that we, women, are natural storytellers …and stories heal souls and minds, stories connect people. This is not new, we've always been like that but the modern world has made many of us forgetful … we forget that the healing and balance we seek comes from the simple joy of creating and sharing our stories with others … be it a recipe for a delicious meal cooked mindfully, slowly, and with love …… be it a card to a friend describing the soulful music played at that little restaurant in the back-street of somewhere exotic be it a book you are writing, or a painting you are painting ……

My message to you is that … YES YOU CAN … you can rely on your imagination, you can express yourself….. you can give yourself permission to embrace your creative side…… It will make you feel whole again. For way too long we have danced to the tune of others, hidden our creative voices, felt powerless… not good enough …. So, let me say from the roof tops, it is time to RISE WOMAN RISE … and tell your story, create new patterns in your life, start that project you've been dreaming about, compose that song, change your career, learn a new language, challenge yourself, do not postpone, start now.

This workbook can be used as a starting point, a place to share your stories as the imagination is creating them, around the kitchen table, in the village hall, or on holiday, with old or new friends, relaxing, gossiping, giggling, over a cup of tea, with a bunch of pens, paints and bits and pieces to hand ... sharing feelings, sharing emotions ....learning from each other and inspiring each other.

Or you can simply enjoy the workbook wherever you are ... on a train commuting to work, during your "ME" time be it 10 minutes or 20 or more, during the school holidays, or simply while you are travelling to take in and write about new places. For it is your travelling companion..... the perfect space to store your memories, to stick your mementos from the trip ... that tram ticket, or ticket to that fascinating museum, or the leaflet from that beautiful castle you want to remember, or the unusual bill from that cafe on the beach you cannot forget, or the place where you will start that book you've been dreaming about or that short story, or start drawing and doodling randomly .. or .. .or ....

It is your space .. and your space only .... Use it.....enjoy it ...

"MAY YOU FIND YOUR
INNER SPARKLE AND
INVITE CREATIVITY INTO
YOUR LIFE"

THE COLOURING IN SECTION

Colouring-in is a relaxing pastime. It really does not matter what colouring materials you have to hand at home ... just start with whatever you have ... colouring pens, juicy pens, watercolours, acrylics, oil pastels, watercolour pencils .. or any combination of them. I also invite you to continue the lines of the designs ... use your imagination.

Colouring-in helps reduce anxiety and stress, it is a form of creative meditation and it can improve your sleeping pattern. I write this from my own personal experience - I know it is true for me.

Colouring-in helps you to understand what colours work well with other colours. Without focusing on it you start to build your own colouring vocabulary - the language of how colours link together in ways that make the whole painting look lovely. It's a brilliant way of developing your colour painting ability and affinity.

Time and time again people ask me ... how come that I am so committed to creative self expression, where does all of this come from?

Believe it or not, everything started 15 years ago. My fiancé brought me a present - an A4 "painting by numbers" set - you can buy them in most art shops in England. This really was the beginning of my creative arts journey. Painting by numbers helped me to escape from the harsh world of my youth - all the pain and despair disappeared when I was in the meditative state of mind that comes when you are painting by numbers - and colouring-in.

So, start colouring-in but also continue the designs in your own, very special way. Simply continue the lines and cover the whole page. The design will be absolutely unique, it will have your energy and imprint!

THE COLLAGING SECTION

What happens when you open a new magazine? You see a great photo, a brilliant colour, an interesting shape, a beautiful use of a word, a set of words in harmony? Perfect! This is exactly where your creation of a collage starts. From a stack of magazines, a tube of glue, a palette knife, a journal and ... this is it! .... You are ready to go! ....But just before you start, a little history...

Collage and collaging was accepted as a legitimate art form by the "traditional" arts movement in the early years of the 20th century when it was practiced by many artists including influential ones like Picasso, Braque and Matisse. Yet the art of collage has way longer roots, dating back hundreds of years, even thousands. Denied the opportunity to paint or to sculpt, often well to do ladies embraced self-expression with their own equivalents of scissors and glue and created their own inventive and imaginative pieces portraying life as it was for them.

Today, we live ever more busy and materialistic lives and our inner selves often lay abandoned, forgotten, neglected by the values of modern life. And so a part of our souls suffers ...a part of ourselves feels a deep need to search, to share, to reconnect with the symbols of ancient times, to discover what lies within us.

Storytelling through images moves these pressures aside, it allows us to go into deeper places in our mind, helping us to explore things that are deeply buried within us, stories that are sometimes hard to express through only words.

Visual languages existed before humans had formed sentences! Collaging takes the oldest form of language, pictures, and blends it with the youngest, words, to produce images that truly bring storytelling alive.

Be prepared to be amazed by the images you create, by the way you combine words and pictures on paper, remembering always that the visual language you are embracing is the oldest language of all times.

To help you make your way into the practice of collage I have suggested nine collaging ideas, including some Japanese haiku poems, as a source of collaging inspiration. Enjoy!

THE CREATIVE WRITING SECTION

Journaling, the creative writing form I use in my workbook, is a really pleasurable relaxation for today.... and it will be our memories of the future.

I've been journaling on and off for many years, filling up journal after journal, a dozen or more a year, with so many personal stories, life plans, life experiences, thoughts on so many matters, recipes, moving quotations I came across, drawings I usually made after supper, poems I read again and again, lists of books I loved or music or documentaries I valued. I can honestly say that journaling is a part of my life, a part that I cannot imagine not doing..... it's who I am, it's who we all are, a vast store of events.......I just have the habit of turning the store into my future memories.

Journaling is almost as old as writing itself. The age-old habit of penning our innermost thoughts and recollections of happenings has provided historians time and again with unique, invaluable, truly illuminating insights into the way a person and we as societies have evolved and existed – the unpublished gossip, the plotting, the unknown loves and so much more. And for our families who come after us, when

we pass them on, the journals can provide answers that unlock their understanding of family history.

Journaling has proved to be useful in other ways too. Literary icon Virginia Woolf was not only a masterful letter-writer but also a dedicated journal keeper. As her husband observes in the introduction to her collected journals, A Writer's Diary, Woolf's journaling was "a method of practicing or trying out the art of writing."

So, however you come to view the practice of keeping a journal - a pleasurable way of creating your future memories - a way of enjoyably practicing the art of writing - a way of reflecting on events of the time, or of putting things into a better perspective - journaling is a wonderful, important pastime.

And one last very important thing to remember. Journaling, the simple gesture of putting pen on paper and expressing oneself, once again reduces stress, benefits the immune system, keeps memory and mind sharp, boosts our moods and heightens our emotional responses - a truly wonderful way of caring for ourselves.

As a way of easing your introduction to journaling I have suggested a dozen prompts for you to have a go at writing on. These "prompts" switch off your logical brain and allow your imagination to flow.....so that you become completely engrossed in your journalling subject, switching off the noise of the day.

Reading, just like journalling has been part of my life for a very long time. I hope that my book suggestions will bring you hours of joyful reading. learning, exploring ....

ENJOY YOUR CREATIVE JOURNEY!

"The best time to plant a tree was 20 years ago. The second best time is ... now!" – Chinese proverb

THE MONTH OF SPROUTING BUDS

Book resource: "Happy" by Derren Brown
Why more or less everything is absolutely fine

"NO ONE CAN EVER TAKE YOUR
MEMORIES FROM YOU – EACH DAY IS A
NEW BEGINNING, MAKE GOOD
MEMORIES EVERY DAY"
Catherine Pulsifier

Embrace change

COLLAGE PROMPT - celebrating spring

Choose images and printed words and create a collage that speaks to you of spring, of what spring means to you - maybe an awakening after a long winter, or a celebration of new life, or a new beginning for the natural world around us..... be inspired by a Japanese Haiku by Issa

"In the city fields, contemplating cherry-trees, strangers are like friends"

Journal

WRITING PROMPT - I have a dream

Imagine you are journaling your thoughts on this subject after watching a thought provoking programme on the 1960's civil rights movement in the Southern States of America. Martin Luther King famously said the words "I have a dream". His dream was non materialistic, it was about the rights of a group of citizens to be
equal under the law. What would your non-materialistic dream be?

Don't think too much, and don't look for the perfect words ...just write, write, write for 20 minutes...

Journal

Journal

Invest in yourself

Be an explorer

"Optimism is the faith that leads to achievement; nothing can be done without hope" - Helen Keller

THE MONTH OF FLOWERING

Book recommendation: "Goddess wisdom made easy" - Connect to the power of the sacred feminine through ancient teachings and practices by Taniska

"THE MOST POWERFUL WEAPON IN THE HANDS OF THE OPPRESSOR IS THE MIND OF THE OPPRESSED" – Steve Biko

You can do it

COLLAGE PROMPT - Happy moments
expressed as a collage

Create a collage dedicated to happy moments in your life, to special memories told through images and words that describe them.
Happiness is a wonderful thing, it touches us in the smallest ways............

"Dancing on the wind, Happy feet above the earth, Life is a playground" - Anonymous

Journal

WRITING PROMPT - A letter written to me

Once upon a time, actually ages ago, people used to write letters
to each other by hand, beautifully decorated with drawings, collages,
mini paintings. It was a pleasure to receive them, it was a pleasure
to send them. Write that letter to yourself - as a reflective journal
entry, the words you would love to receive from your best friend
about you... compassionate, loving, optimistic, empowering, uplifting.

Journal

Journal

Stay curious

Draw a pink elephant

"Maybe my passion is nothing special but at least it's mine" – Tove Jansson

MONTH OF MEADOWS

Book recommendation: "The women who run with the wolves" by Clarissa Pinkola Estes

"GO OUT INTO THE WOODS, GO OUT. IF YOU DON'T GO OUT IN THE WOODS NOTHING WILL EVER HAPPEN AND YOUR LIFE WILL NEVER BEGIN"- Clarissa Pinkola Estes

Draw a pink elephant

COLLAGE PROMPT - Mother Earth

Mother Earth, the spirit of the natural world.... forgiving, crying, celebrating, rebelling, teaching, loving. Create a collage dedicated to what does the concept of Mother Earth mean to you!

"One flower, On the cliffside, Nodding at the canyon" - Jack Kerouac

Journal

WRITING PROMPT - That person was truly inspirational

(People come into our lives for a reason, a season or a day)
Enjoy the memories of people you knew while you reflect on this question. Look back at your life and write for 20 minutes about the people who really influenced your life and why. What was it that they did or inspired you to do.......

Journal

Journal

Believe in your talents!

Use your imagination

"For most of history, Anonymous was a woman"
— Virginia Woolf

MONTH OF HARVEST

Book recommendation: "Three daughters of Eve"
by Elif Shafak

"AND THOUSE WHO WERE SEEN DANCING WERE THOUGHT TO BE INSANE BY THOSE WHO COULD NOT HEAR THE MUSIC" – Friedrich Nietzche

You are a brave soul

COLLAGE PROMPT - Shades of blue

Flip through your stack of magazines and create a collage that focuses on the colour blue, on the various shades of blue. This colour allows self expression and personal creativity to flourish, is associated with the throat chakra and responsible for the free flow of communication at all levels.

Journal

WRITING PROMPT - The road less travelled

Reflect with a pen in one hand and a cup of something in the other ......
was there a moment in time when you chose to take a road less travelled,
to do something that had no guaranteed outcome, that was not the easiest
but that appealed to you, something that brought you out of your comfort
zone? Write a journal entry about these moments and what you learned
about yourself?

Journal

Journal

Live a meaningful life

You are a brave soul

"Nothing great was ever achieved without enthusiasm" - Ralph Waldo Emerson

MONTH OF WARMTH

Book recommendation: "The Magician in Lhasa" by David Richie

"PART OF THE ACT OF CREATING IS IN DISCOVERING YOUR OWN KIND. THEY ARE EVERYWHERE. BUT DON'T LOOK FOR THEM IN THE WRONG PLACES." – Henry Miller

Read about Frida Kahlo

COLLAGE PROMPT - The richness of autumn

Autumn, the harvest, falling leaves, abundance of crops and fruits, smoky bonfires, warming drinks... create your own visual representation of what autumn means to you, your feelings, the memories of that rich time of year.

"On a leafless branch, A crow comes to rest, Autumn nightfall" - Basho

Journal

WRITING PROMPT – Slow down

(We run, we move faster and faster, and notice less and less)

Take a stroll in the part of your town or village that you like. Deliberately walk slowly, look around you, stop when something you see you hadn't noticed before. Take in the scents, the sounds (you hadn't heard that bird for a long time), the different architectures, the different front gardens, the signs that you hadn't noticed before – absorb them. And then stop in a cafe and write a journal entry about the experience, what really surprised you?

Journal

Journal

Start to de-clutter

Love yourself

"A symbol is an indefinite expression with many meanings, pointing to something not easily defined and therefore not fully known." Carl Jung

MONTH OF FRUITS

Book recommendation: "Autobiography of a yogi" by Paramahansa Yogananda

"I'VE LEARND THAT PEOPLE WILL FORGET WHAT YOU SAID, PEOPLE WILL FORGET WHAT YOU DID, BUT THEY WILL NEVER FORGET HOW YOU MADE THEM FEEL" – Maya Angelou

What is your creative dream?

COLLAGE PROMPT - A collage of Winter

Winter is a season, but it is also a feeling, also a pastiche of images. It is a word but what does that word mean to you ... and what is the visual representation of that word......could it be raindrops on the window, snowdrops, colour white, shades of white...........

"The snow of yesterday, That felt like cherry blossom, Is water once again"
- Gozan

Journal

WRITING PROMPT – The natural world affects the way we are

(Nature responds to the way that we interact with it – and we also respond to the landscape around us – but how)

How does the landscape around you influence your mood and your life? Write a journal entry, write continuously for 20 minutes, write intuitively on what makes you feel good about the natural world – in real detail (fields are one thing but fields of poppies, or lavender, or cereals with skylarks overhead or the wild hedgerows or t…..)– and why.

Journal

Journal

Who is your favourite painter?

What does slowing down mean to you?

"Clear out what doesn't serve you in order to bring in, the life you truly want" - Carrie Anne Moss

MONTH OF VINTAGE

Book recommendation: "When the drummers were women" by Layne Redmond

" THE MAIN THING IS TO BE MOVED, TO LOVE, TO KNOW, TO TREMBLE, TO LIVE" - Auguste Rodin

Be bold! Be free! Be truthful!

COLLAGE PROMPT - Mountains that reach as high as the clouds

Mountains ... what do they represent for you, what do they say to you ... express visually and with words a collage describing how you view mountains, the colour(s) that you associate with them......and be inspired by the poem

"Mountain beautiful, The moon watching, Down on you, Birds flying over you" – Unknown author

Journal

WRITING PROMPT - Imagination -
I'm going to write a story

Let your imagination run wild .... Imagine that ... you have a tail and a pair of beautiful long ears. What kind of world do you live in? What do you see around you? Do you have a family? What do you have to eat? Where do you sleep and on what? What does your reality look like? Are you on planet Earth? Another planet? And what are you doing today? Let it all go, smile, giggle, invent the seemingly ridiculous in a fun journal entry.

Journal

Journal

Look at the world around you in wonderment

Dress up in all the colours of the rainbow

"The important thing is to create. Nothing else matters, creation is all." - Pablo Picasso

MONTH OF FOG

Book recommendation: "Work and love" by Tove Jansson

"THE AIM OF ART IS TO REPRESENT NOT THE OUTWARDS APPEARANCE OF THINGS BUT THEIR INWARD SIGNIFICANCE." – Aristotle

Laughter is the best medicine

COLLAGE PROMPT - About the moon

The moon – is it for you just a beautiful object that shines at night, or is it a thing that makes you wonder what else is out there, who could be out there, could we really be the only intelligent beings to exist among the stars ... what does that mean to you?

"At the crescent moon, The silence, Enters the heart" – Chiyo ni

WRITING PROMPT - Books

A world without books!!!! I cannot even imagine it. Write a journal entry on the book from your childhood, or from later on in your life, that you would love to read again? Why does that particular book have such an important place in your life? Do you remember when you first read it? Write for 20 minutes ...

Journal

Journal

Take time off your phone

Love yourself

"I cannot help considering it a sign of talent that I do not give it up, though I can get nobody to take an interest in my efforts" - Fanny Mendelssohn

MONTH OF WINTRY WEATHER

Book recommendation: "There is nothing wrong with you" by Cheri Huber

"EVERY DAY, THINK AS YOU WAKE UP ...
TODAY I AM FORTUNATE TO BE ALIVE,
I HAVE A PRECIOUS HUMAN LIFE, I AM
NOT GOING TO WASTE IT." – Dalai Lama

Invite yourself for a visit to an art gallery

COLLAGE PROMPT - Create a collage for poetry or a poem

Poetry is not only for the poets but for all of us.... And how you compose a poem does not have to be just words, the magic of poems can be expressed as images and words, the whole collage poem coming alive in front of you. Try collaging any poem you like and see what I mean – or take William Wordsworth's "I Wandered Lonely as a Cloud"- how would you make it as a collage?

"I read poetry, In a mansion tucked away, Among massive pines" – Calvin Olsen

Journal

WRITING PROMPT - Poems

There is something peaceful and meditative about reading a poem ... or listening to a poem being recited .... Do you have a favourite poem? If you do, write it down .... slowly..... letter ....by letter, saying the words in your own mind, enjoying the movement of the pen on the paper. If you don't have a favourite poem, use one created by Hafez, the famous Iranian poet or Wordsworth. Write down one of their poems slowly, a few times - then turn the journal upside down and write the same again slowly, thinking about the words ... it really helps you to connect with the words and the meaning, silencing the outside and heightening your peace within.

Journal

Journal

Combine wonder with imagination

Take yourself for a walk in the woods

When times are distorted, harsh, noisy, confusing, there is more and more the need for calm, reflection, humility.

MONTH OF SNOW

Book recommendation: "The truth will set you free" by Alice Miller

"CREATIVITY IS AN ORGAN THAT IMPROVES WITH USE AND WHEN FULLY ENGAGED IS DIFFICULT TO WEAR OUT"- Robert Genn

What are your values?

COLLAGE PROMPT - Freedom

Create a visual representation of what freedom means to you

Journal

WRITING PROMPT - Imagination

Create a short story using the prompts below.

The fact that you are here means …………………….

How many times do I have to tell you that imagination….

I will always remember the frozen train wagons when ….

In those times we used to imagine that ……………..

And suddenly ………………………………………………………..

Journal

Journal

Time changes your perspective

Yes you can

"Life is going to be tough, but I am going to be tougher." - Malala Yousafzai

MONTH OF RAIN

Book recommendation: "Sane new world" - Ruby Wax

BELIEVING IN YOURSELF IS A
NECESSARY THING IN ORDER TO
SUCCEED IN ANYTHING YOU DO BUT IT
DOES NOT HELP MUCH WITHOUT A
DEDICATED PRACTICE, WITHOUT
PERSEVERANCE.

Life is a mixed media collage

COLLAGE PROMPT- A day in my life

Create a collage using images and words describing ... a day in your life

Journal

WRITING PROMPT - That day ....

It was an early December morning when .....

After so many years I am wondering if ....

It does not mean that ...... but I want you to understand ....

Maybe you have or maybe you haven't thought of all the way that day ...

Changes came out of the blue and now ....

Journal

Journal

Believe in yourself

You are enough

MONTH OF WIND

"GENUINE COURAGE IS DOING SOMETHING THAT NEEDS DOING THAT YOU DON'T QUITE THHINK YOU HAVE …..THE COURAGE TO DO BUT THAT YOU KEEP ON DOING REGARDLESS." – ChurchiLl

Pay attention to how you feel

COLLAGE PROMPT - Creativity means...

Create a collage of images and words related to the word .... Creativity and what does it mean to you.

Journal

WRITING PROMPT – the unexpected word

Continue the sentences and create your own story based on the prompts below.

Little did I know when I woke up this morning that ....

And listening about this reminded me that ....

Although it was a long time ago I felt as if ....

And this is where my story starts for real .... Listen ....

Journal

Journal

Journal

Journal

Journal

Journal

Journal

Printed in Poland
by Amazon Fulfillment
Poland Sp. z o.o., Wrocław

59212635R00087

First published in 2017

© text: Myrddin ap Dafydd

Prose translated from the Welsh by Susan Walton.
© translation: Susan Walton 2017

Ballads translated from the Welsh by Mike Jenkins.
© translation: Mike Jenkins 2017

© images: Dorry Spikes

Publishers: Gwasg Carreg Gwalch

ISBN: 978-1-84527-600-3

Published with the financial support of the
Welsh Books Council.

Cover and inside images: Dorry Spikes
Cover design: Eleri Owen

Published and printed by Gwasg Carreg Gwalch,
12 Iard yr Orsaf, Llanrwst, Wales LL26 0EH
tel: 01492 642031
email: books@carreg-gwalch.com
website: www.carreg-gwalch.com

The Story of Wales

Histories and Ballads

Myrddin ap Dafydd   Images: Dorry Spikes

Histories translated by Susan Walton
Ballads translated by Mike Jenkins

Thanks

Aside from general reading (and here I should refer to the fantastic Darganfod Hanes Cymru volumes 1–4 by Robert M. Morris, Catrin Stevens and Geraint H. Jenkins), I received excellent help with some of the individual stories and poems and I'm very grateful to these people:

The Red Kite – the company of Iwan Llwyd and Olwen Edwards' Barcud Coch project
Where is Pengwern tonight? – interpretations by Professor Geraint Gruffydd and Tecwyn Ifan
Gruffudd in Chester prison – Ysgol Aberdaron
Gwenllïan – Ysgol Porth Tywyn
Moel y Don – Ysgol y Felinheli
The Children of the Princes – Ieuan Wyn, Bethesda
Praise the Lark – the traditional song 'Marwnad yr Hedydd', Rod Barrar, Merêd and Nia Watcyn Powell
Carreg y Gwalch – Emrys Evans, Blaenau Ffestiniog and old Llanrwst storytellers
Old Woman and Wynn o Wydir – old Llanrwst storytellers and Ysgol Ysbyty Ifan
The Pirate's Island – Ysgol Trelewis
A Press Gang on Bardsey – rhiw.com
Destroying the Chartist Mural – an article in Golwg
The little Maid of Penrhyn Castle – a Welsh attendant in that bedroom
Tearful Owen – R. E. Jones, Llanrwst (Owen's brother)
5 a.m. in Senghenydd – John 'Clogs' Jones, Llanllwni landlord
'Moto Ni' – Geraint Jones and Ysgol Trefor
Christmas in France, 1914 – christmastruce.co.uk
Ysgwrn farm – Gerald Williams
Women Marching – Llyfr y Ganrif, ed. Gwyn Jenkins
The Tirdyrys Fishermen – Gareth Neigwl and Griffith Thomas' Diary, 1933
Song of Lydia Hughes – Nic Reed, Rhydyclafdy (her nephew)
Hole under the stairs – shadowpoetry.com
Ballad of Llangyndeyrn – Hywel Rees' history,
        Sefyll yn y Bwlch: Brwydr Llangyndeyrn 1960–1965
On the 'Miga-moga' – Nant Gwrtheyrn's heritage department

I also wish to gratefully acknowledge being granted a Writer's Bursary from Literature Wales in 2013 to work on this collection in Welsh.

Dedicated to
the present and future children of Wales
who enjoy a good story
from their country's treasury

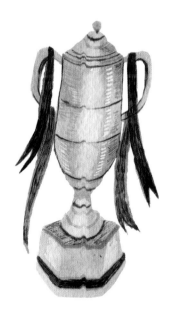

Contents

A Word at the Start

Travelling Wales has been part of my life – journeying to all parts to visit family and friends, to enjoy the National Eisteddfod, going on holiday, or taking pictures for some book or other. Travelling the country has also been part of my work as a poet, including visiting many schools in every corner of Wales.

On these trips, I've remembered, or heard, stories. And in time, when we arrive in a new valley or a new area, my children have got used to asking the question – 'What's the story of this place?'

Stories are told for many reasons. Amusement, for starters. Certainly, enjoying listening to a story is important. Stories also tell us something about historical characters and demonstrate that there's more to the country than meets the eye – or the camera lens. The audience – they're important too. That, and the time to tell the tale properly.

The dentist's chair is not one of my favourite places in the world. When I was a child, we went from Llanrwst to a dentist in Llandudno. That's half an hour in which to anticipate what will happen in that chair. Dad would often relate stories about Llywelyn or Glyndŵr on the journey, and end with the line: 'When I'm sitting in the dentist's chair, I imagine Glyndŵr supporting one of my arms, and Llywelyn holding the other.' I still think of that line when I've got to go to the dentist today!

The last time I saw T. Llew Jones, the children's author, my wife and three of my children were with me. Straight off, T. Llew said to we adults that it was the children he wanted to talk to that day. He started to tell them a story about a farm dog. This dog got up from in front of the fire and went out into the farmyard. He saw the pig in its sty and heard it grunting. The dog tried to grunt like the pig. He went on to the cowshed and listened to the cow lowing. He tried to low like a cow. He passed the henhouse where a hen was clucking loudly as she'd just laid an egg. The dog tried clucking. On his way back across the farmyard, he spotted the farmer coming out of the house. The dog tried to curry favour by showing off his new skills by grunting and lowing and clucking. 'What's the matter with you?' asked the farmer. 'You're no good to me unless you can bark like a dog. Get out of my sight, you stupid dog!' And that's the story T. Llew left with the children.

At the start of the Six Nations competition in 2005, the Wales rugby team coach at the time, Mike Ruddock, gave each member of the squad a big black file after one training session, 'I want you all to read its contents,' he said. No, the file didn't contain rugby tactics – it was a collection of stories from the history of Wales. That season, that squad beat every other country and secured the first Grand Slam for Wales for 27 years.

The more of our stories that are out there in the world, the more the world will know our country and people. We will also be prepared to deal with current issues and will be able to see more clearly what the future may hold. A knowledge of our history is like a penetrating X-ray, letting us see through the soft flesh of today's news to the bare bones beneath. We will understand today's problems better – but, more importantly, we will know where the answers can be found.

There are several ways of presenting a story. I remember going to see the Celyn valley, now under the waters of Llyn Celyn reservoir, before the dam across the Tryweryn river was complete – I remember seeing the big yellow machines carving out the valley, demolishing old farmhouses and pulling trees up by their roots. The images have stayed in my memory. Those images still tell the story for me.

In my early school years, I pestered the teacher over and over for a story from one special volume. It had a red cover, and was called *Ein Hen, Hen Hanes* (Our Old, Old History) – and I can still hear her voice reading chapters about Caradog and Gruffudd ap Cynan.

When I go round schools in Wales, as often as not I seek out a story about that particular area and start the session by telling it to the class. Having heard the story, they set to afterwards to create a ballad or poem based on the tale. When they make a fair copy of their words, they often illustrate an element of their story to go with their verses.

The idea of this book is something similar. Over the years, I've heard and collected stories. In presenting them here to you, I've written poems too. The artist Dorry Spikes has created pictures to go with the tales and poems. Maybe some of the poems will be sung before too long – yes, there is more than one way to convey a story. But the intention, always, is to give you enjoyment, and to empower you.

Myrddin ap Dafydd

The Red Kite

If there is any bird that can be called the 'bird of Wales', the red kite surely is that creature. It nests in the ancient oak woodland and can be seen high above coastal marshes, upland farmland and wild places in all parts of Wales. Its forked tail makes it easily recognisable.

'Kite!' A common enough cry when someone spots one and points it out. There'll always be excitement and wonder in the voice. And with good reason.

The red kite was within a whisper of disappearing from our country at one time. They were persecuted by gamekeepers, and their rare eggs collected, and at one point during the last century only one hen-bird remained in mid-Wales. But farmers, local people and societies came to the rescue by determinedly protecting the birds' nests. Gradually, numbers increased and its range extended throughout Wales again.

More than any other bird, the red kite is an inspiration for the art of survival in Wales. It has become one of the symbols of the nation's endurance.

Land of the Red Kite

Where the light of ancient times
Comes in the morning to the mountains,
Resting upon bears' and wolves' bones,
Tracing the paths of our ancestors:
    That is the land of the red kite.

Where the sun upon stone circles
Creates fingers out of the shadows
And weight of the past on a cromlech,
Showing the ring's true worth:
    That is the land of the red kite.

Where the oak, in its soundness,
Makes such a solid shield
And there's music in hammer and chisel
Closing the gaps in stone walls:
    That is the land of the red kite.

Place of the valleys forking narrow,
Place of the colourful acres,
Where, in the sky's wide canvas,
There's a shivering flight of feathers:
    That is the land of the red kite.

Land of the lost valleys,
Land of the poisoned winds;
Yet in touch with ancient dreams
Our children learn to fly again:
    This is the land of the red kite.

Cromlechi (Dolmens)

There are the remains of old burial sites, called *cromlechi* (dolmens), the length and breadth of Wales. All that remains to be seen today is a capstone and four or five upright stones supporting its enormous weight. Bodies would have been buried in the *cromlech* and the whole lot would have been covered over with earth and stones.

Over the years, most of the earth mounds disappeared, leaving bare stones. Some of them have interesting names – Pentre Ifan, Maen y Bardd and Carreg Samson. On heathland on the Gower, Glamorgan, there is a *cromlech* with a massive capstone. This stone forms the *cromlech*'s roof and weighs over twenty-five tons! How on earth did ancient people, over four or five thousand years ago, shift such weights?

There's a story behind the name of this very *cromlech*. Its name? Maen Arthur (*Arthur's Stone*). And the story? King Arthur was riding in Carmarthenshire when he noticed that his horse was lame. He dismounted to attend to the troublesome hoof and saw that there was a small stone lodged under the horseshoe. He extracted the stone and tossed it over his shoulder without a second thought. It landed on Gower – and that's the capstone of Maen Arthur! What a giant our Arthur was!

Arthur's Stone

The cromlech Arthur's Stone is huge –
On a hill in Gower it stands,
There are four stones surrounding,
But it is at the peak of the land.

The old legend tells of Arthur
In the Llandeilo area one day,
Riding his magnificent white steed
And visiting a friend on his way.

A stone flew out from a horseshoe
Like an arrow speeding quick,
But Arthur leapt from his saddle
To the ground as the pain struck.

He took the sharp stone in his hand
And flung it over his shoulder;
It flew away over Glamorgan
Took the shape of a table, this boulder.

Twenty-five tons the cromlech weighs,
Which lies upon the hill;
What kind of leader was this
To throw with all his skill?

Finn was a strong man in Ireland,
There was gigantic Hok-Braz in Brittany,
For the Welsh the king was Arthur
And he was indeed mighty!

Standing Stones

On Anglesey, as in many parts of Wales, a number of tall stones stand upright in the ground. These are 'standing stones' and were placed there thousands of years ago. Maybe some of them are signposts, showing the way to somewhere. It's possible that others are gravestones. And some believe that the shadows they cast are a kind of calendar on the ground.

Nobody is really sure of their exact purpose now. They belong to prehistory – before anyone wrote on parchment or on paper. Because there are no written records, stories and legends take root. And that's exactly what has happened with some of these standing stones.

In a field in Llandyfrydog, in the middle of Anglesey, a slightly different stone stands in the shadow of a hedge. There is a large lump at the top of this stone.

At some point, someone imagined that the stone looks like a bent-over man carrying a sack on his back. Then the story grew. The man was a thief who had his eye on the Great Bible in Llandyfrydog church. He reckoned he could get a good price for it if he could steal it. He set out for the church one night but it was a moonlit night.

'Oh, no,' he said. 'Someone might recognize me walking out of the church in the moonlight with the Great Bible in a sack on my back.'

At that, a cloud blotted out the moon. The land was dark and the thief saw his chance. Into the church he went, put the Bible in his sack, and carried it out on his back. As he was sneaking through a nearby field, keeping close to the hedge, the moon came out again.

The thief was caught in the white light of the moon, and the man, the sack, and the Great Bible were turned to stone on the spot. The stone is called Carreg Leidr ('*thief's stone*') and, apparently, every Christmas Eve the Carreg Leidr springs out of the ground and runs three times round the field!

The Stone Thief

In the darkness, dreams of riches;
In the darkness, silent the glebe;
In the darkness, his hands stretching;
In the darkness, the spirit is weak.

Silver moon over fields and church;
Silver moon as every living thing sleeps;
Silver moon over the wide path;
Silver moon and silver he worships.

Hand on the Bible and reciting psalms;
Hand on the Bible, the whispering of charms;
Hand on the Bible and his pocket's full;
Hand on the Bible, so easy to steal.

Sack on his back, running though graveyard;
Sack on his back, jumping over the ditch;
Sack on his back, moonlight's shards;
Sack on his back and heavy's the night.

Weight of prison on his back and neck;
Weight of prison on his manacled feet;
Never again will the stone thief
So readily run and leap.

The Brythons

When the Romans came to Wales, their historians set out to record something of the history of the Brythons – our Celtic ancestors. According to these accounts in Latin, they fished the rivers using lightweight circular boats of wickerwork coated with hide. If you go to Cenarth on the Teifi river or Carmarthen on the Tywi, you may see these small boats – coracles – still in use to this day. The history of our people is woven tightly into the history of the country in which we live.

Coracle on the river

I come in the quiet coracle downstream
Through pools of black and fog of memories;
Harp-notes from willows bending above water
And rocks flanking the blue castle of the river.

Fork of the red kite where the currents rise,
Mane of mountain pony reflected under clear sky,
A barking corgi keeps pigs from the corn
And a Welsh cob dances across stepping-stones.

A light journey with only water-language heard
Telling the story of centuries like spring birds,
Of that first man here, making a wooden round,
Firelight on the banks and a gasp of sound.

The Brythons and the Romans

The Brythons were a branch of the Celtic tribes, living south of the Scottish Highlands, speaking Brythonic. Welsh, Cornish and Breton are derived from Brythonic.

Buddug (*Boudicca*) was a Brython. She was the wife of the chief of the Iceni tribe in eastern Britain, and in 61 AD the chief died. They had no son, but under Brythonic law the chief's wife – Buddug – and her daughters could lead the tribe. It was normal in Celtic culture for women to lead armies too. However, that's not how the Romans saw things – they attacked the tribe's core, whipping Buddug, abusing the girls and occupying Iceni lands.

Buddug and her daughters assembled the Iceni tribe and their neighbours – the Trinovantes – and torched the Roman city of Colchester. A legion of Roman soldiers was sent to oppose them and the Brythons won a great victory in that fight too. The Brythons went on to burn and destroy two other Roman colonies, London and St Albans, before being defeated at the Battle of Watling Street.

On the bank of the Thames in London, across the road from the House of Commons, there is a striking sculpture of a warrior with a spear in one hand, her two rearing warhorses pulling her chariot into battle. With her in the chariot are two young girls.

This is a memorial to Buddug and her daughters.

Buddug speaks

We must, in the land of the Britons,
Be more than mere men.
Not only arrows in our creels,
Swords and spears at the ready,
Not just the fire of hatred
And stones of vengeance,
We need more than words
And their weight in argument.
Fear of losing our good name
Is greater than any fear of dying.
The supple strength to refuse
Flows longer than bleeding wounds.
The iron in our hearts stays
Even though we remain captive.
We must, in the land of the Britons,
Be more than mere men.
Eagles with their sharp talons
Hover over all our doings;
To them our sole purpose
Is to be their carrion.

They steal and claim everything,
Take our country by invasion.
We must rise to face them
Like a stallion lifting hooves.
Rise to their wicked intentions
Like a woman conjuring a spirit.
Rise, thousand upon thousand,
Like the sea with waves surging.
We must, in the land of the Britons,
Be more than mere men.

Caradog

Caradog attacked the Romans bravely when they came to occupy Britain two thousand years ago. He lost many battles, but he never lost heart. He went from tribe to tribe raising armies and bringing hope to his people. He fought hard in the mountains of Wales, leading the local Britons. But in the end, Rome's armies were too overwhelming and too well-disciplined, and Caradog was caught.

It was decided to take him and his family all the way to Rome to be displayed to the crowds – to show that he, the fearless leader, had finally been defeated by Caesar's army. Caradog and his family were paraded in chains through the streets and then presented to a throned Caesar. Ordered to bow before the emperor, Caradog remained standing, saying that he too was a king and would not bow to any man. Caesar and the Romans respected Caradog's courage – he was not killed, but neither did he return to the land of the Britons.

This was my favorite story when I was in the Infant School in Llanrwst. It is a story about the will to persevere – although the battle may be lost, we must believe we have not been completely defeated.

Caradog before Caesar

You are opulent, Caesar, rich pearls
To pay your armies of the world.

You are secure, Caesar, from Spanish iron
Each sword is shining.

You are popular, Caesar, crowds praise
Your ventures and are amazed.

You are powerful, Caesar, foot-soldiers tread
In legions to carry out bloodshed.

You're resplendent on a throne like a god,
Life and death decided at your nod.

Away from the round huts, I am a prisoner,
Away from the goats and oats, land of my father
Our fort on the ridge and all our weapons
Could not halt your steely precision.
I kept faith in the mountain roads
But your ranks crushed us like toads.
You may own rocks and trees in every valley –
It is all taken from the likes of me.

You are successful, Caesar, I have lost
The day, my history. But at what cost,
To reduce a people to misery
Who possess one language and one country?

I refuse to bow, Caesar,
You can do what you will with me,

But there's a spirit within me
Cannot be broken by any powerful army.

Roads, Forts, Markets

In our time, the busy M4 motorway leads from the Severn bridges through the ancient kingdoms of Gwent and Glamorgan and onward to the west. One hundred and fifty years earlier, a railway was built to connect more or less the same towns and cities. Even before that, there were drovers' roads and roads built by the Normans for their armies to invade our lands. But the first to create roads reaching into Wales from the east were the Romans.

Gwent and Glamorgan were Silurian lands in Roman times. These Britons have been described as dark-complexioned, fierce and determined. They were effective soldiers and robustly protected their lands from falling under Roman rule. For thirty years, between 43 AD and 75 AD, the Silures kept the strength of Rome at bay in south-east Wales through a long series of hard and bloody battles.

In the end, the Romans gained the upper hand, but only by sending thousands of troops into the area to defeat the Silures. To retain these lands, the Romans built a massive riverside fortress at Caerleon, on the Usk. This became home to up to 5,500 troops until around the year 483. It was one of Roman Britain's main fortresses and there were roads linking it with several smaller forts to the north and east, and alongside every river throughout south Wales – the Taff, Ebbw, Neath, Tawe, Loughor, and Tywi.

On the road eastwards from Caerleon, the Romans built a market town on a 44-acre site at Caer-went. This was the largest commercial centre in Wales and its remains are the best-preserved in Britain. Overall, the town walls are intact, although they have fallen into disrepair. One can walk around the town today and marvel at the Roman walls and towers and the remains of a temple, bathhouses, markets, grand houses and shops. Caer-went is historic, as there was not a single town in Wales before Roman times.

The technique of the Romans has been repeated by many invaders down the centuries – roads to transport armies into Wales, forts and military castles built, and then markets created to regulate the local economy.

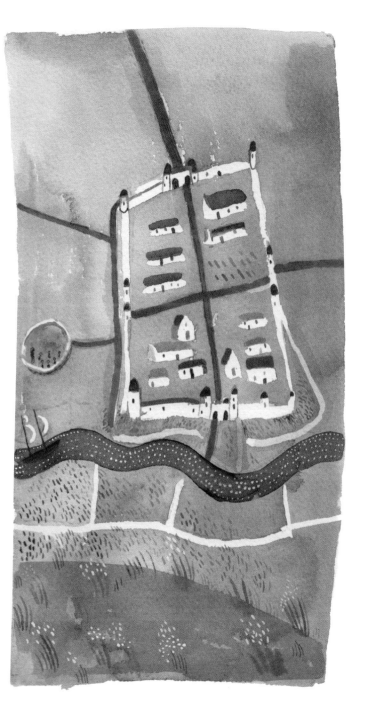

Caer-went

A quiet road leads there today
Between still fields, through the trees,
Cars sparkling in their spots:
Plenty of time on our hands
To search for remains of the settlement.

Walking the dog around the circle of walls
We cross the stile beside the tower;
Here was once a busy market-place
Full of food and provisions for the province,
Money in the pockets of the Silures.

We peer at plaques as we go back
And step over baths and houses,
There's Latin on the old stones
Inside a church and weapons
Between fragments of tiles and vases.

From tranquillity of this strange valley
We turn and return to the world of today,
Drive back along the motorway
Passing buses, vans and lorries,
Speeding westward on whirling wheels.

The Age of the Saints

Wales in the sixth century was a time of church-building, striving for peace and remembering what's best in life. This was the Age of the Saints. The emphasis was on preaching, spreading the word of Christ and living simply – reading, writing, working the land and praying.

Beuno, Illtyd, Teilo, Dewi – these are names of some of the saints. Are they familiar? Look at a map of Wales and pretty quickly you'll discover place names that include the names of these saints. And what about the '*llan*' that often precedes the name of the saint?

On their travels, the saints would establish small churches in lonely spots. Their followers would create a village around the church – and that's the *llan*. The *llan* would be named after the saint that founded it. There are more than 430 places beginning 'Llan' in Wales.

What a lot of saints! They weren't all Welsh either. Some came from Brittany, Cornwall and Ireland in small boats made of wood and hide. This was the age of the Celtic saints and of large, stone Celtic crosses which show elaborate, highly-skilled decoration. But although these men – and women too – were pious, they were adventurous and brave; there are amazing stories about their determined spirit.

Footpaths lead to the Llan

Llanbadarn Fawr, Llanbadarn Fynydd,
Llanddewi'r Cwm, Llan-gair, Llanefydd,
Llanfihangel Genau'r Glyn, Llanbedrog,
Llangernyw, Llanddwyn and Llangrannog,

> *From beach to valley, for woman and man,*
> *Every footpath leads to the Llan.*

Llanfihangel Rhos-y-corn, Llansannan,
And Llanfair Nant-y-gof, Llanrian,
Llantrisant and Llanrug, Llanuwchllyn,
Llandrindod, Llan San Siôr, Llanwddyn,

Llandudno, Llannor and Llanelli,
Llangurig, Llangwm and Llangybi,
Llanddaniel-fab, Llan-rhos, Llanfabon,
Llanbrynmair and Llangwyryfon,

Llandŵ, Llangatwg, Llanybydder,
And Llangristiolus and Llangywer,
Llanrwst, Llan-wern and Llanymawddwy,
Llanwrtyd, Llansanffraid Glyndyfrdwy,

Llangefni, Llan-ffwyst Fawr, Llangeitho,
Llangwnnadl, Llannarth and Llandeilo,
Llanilltud Faerdref and Llanfigel,
Llanllŷr, Llangatwg Feibion Afel,

Llandysul, Llanfihangel Ystrad,
Llanddoged, Llandyfân, Llanddingad,
Llanddewibrefi, Llanddeiniolen,
Llandyrnog, Llan-y-cefn, Llangollen,

> *From beach to valley, for woman and man,*
> *Every footpath leads to the Llan.*

Saint David (Dewi Sant)

The cathedral at St David's stands in Glyn Rhosyn, a quiet hollow below the town's streets. Saint David's simple monastery was here, on the bank of a small river fringed with lush vegetation. Water was sacred to the ancient

Celts and very important to the saints of the Celtic Church too.

The saints made medicines from herbs. People would travel far to listen to David preaching, and to receive a healing. In Welsh, many plants are named after saints – the Virgin Mary in particular. For example, a type of dog-rose that grows along Pembrokeshire's coast is 'Dewi's rose' in Welsh.

Sometimes fugitives would seek refuge with the saints. There is an ancient earth embankment across the St David's Peninsula. According to tradition, once this – the *'Monk's Ditch'* – was crossed, no one had the right to harm a fugitive because by then they were under Saint David's patronage.

Glyn Rhosyn

Between honeysuckle and ferns of Mary
Take the old way to Glyn Rhosyn;
Wearing sandals through the hay
Between honeysuckle and ferns of Mary.
Approaching the cairn and relic,
Sensing the world beyond the promontory;
Between honeysuckle and ferns of Mary
Take the old way to Glyn Rhosyn.

There beyond the yew is water
To wash away dust and ashes of lives;
Although the sound is loud and drowning
There's hope beyond fading eyes
To capture a fountain above the tides,
There beyond the yew is cleansing
To wash away dust and ashes of lives.

The way we take we cannot reach
Into the valley past the Monk's Ditch;
With the fall of land to those waves.
The way we take we cannot reach
To find Dewi's white roses,
Catch sight of Ramsey's black rocks;
The way we take we cannot reach
Into the valley past the Monk's Ditch.

Wales and the Welsh

There was plenty of warring in Wales after the Romans left the country, as the native Welsh attempted to defend their lands against invaders from both east and west. Children in Wales learn the important difference in spelling between *Cymru* and *Cymry* – *Cymru* with an '*u*' is the country, and *Cymry* with a '*y*' are the natives of that country. But essentially the two are the same word, and there is no other country in the world where the name of the land and that of the people who live there are the same.

The word '*Cymru*' is the plural of '*Cymro*', which is 'a person who shares the same locality'. Names have a history, and in the sixth century the people of that time started to use the word '*Cymru*' for both themselves and their country. It is a welcoming and peaceful name, meaning 'people living together'. The last of the Romans had left the British Isles in the year 410 and the native Welsh were not used to defending themselves. When droves of foreigners arrived from several directions by sea to scout out what these islands had to offer, they were welcomed at first, but the Welsh didn't know who they were at that time. Many of them came from Germany and other parts of north-western Europe – they were the Saxons, and in time it became clear that they were dangerous enemies.

'Welsh' was the name the Saxons gave to the *Cymry*. In old Saxon it meant 'alien people, different people'. That's a sign of their audacity! They came over to the land of the native Welsh and called us strangers in our own land. The name 'Saxon', by the way, comes from the word *saex*, which is a slender, long, sharp knife: the Saxons' favoured weapon.

During this period Gwrtheyrn (*Vortigern*) was king of the Brythons – an unfortunate king who made a serious error. Before fleeing to Snowdonia and Nant Gwrtheyrn, his castle and capital were in south-eastern England but his lands were being threatened by the Picts, a warlike people from Scotland. What Gwrtheyrn did was to make an arrangement with two brothers who were mercenaries – Hengist and Hors. They were aggressive Saxons from northern Germany, and with their help Gwrtheyrn and his men managed to defeat the Picts. To reward these wandering privateers, Gwrtheyrn gave them land on the Isle of Thanet in south-east England. But once they had possession of the land, the Saxons were greedy for more and more of the country.

Before long, the Saxons Hengist and Hors were at war with Gwrtheyrn's armies. Hors was killed, but more and more Saxons arrived from Germany, capturing more and more land. Hengist had a beautiful daughter called Rhonwen

(*Rowena*), and Gwrtheyrn fell for her. Hengist agreed to give his daughter in marriage to Gwrtheyrn on condition that the Saxons got the whole of the kingdom of Kent to themselves. Gwrtheyrn agreed to the deal.

But still the Saxons fought for more land. Following years of war, Hengist reached another deal with Gwrtheyrn. To celebrate the newly-won peace between the native Welsh and the Saxons, Hengist organised a huge May Day feast on Salisbury Plain, where Stonehenge can be seen.

As it says in an old book on the history of the Welsh, even though the Saxons spoke in a friendly fashion, they thought like wolves. Hengist instructed each Saxon to conceal a sharp knife about his person, and on the command, 'Hey, draw your *saexes*!' each was to produce his knife and kill the nearest Welshman.

And so it was. Three hundred leaders of the ancient Welsh arrived and were seated at the tables alternately with three hundred Saxon soldiers. To all appearances all were unarmed – by agreement. They began the feasting but then Hengist shouted, 'Hey, draw your *saexes*!'

The Saxons drew their knives and attacked the Welshmen, and so the killing started. Hengist had instructed that Gwrtheyrn be seized rather than killed, so he could buy his freedom and thereby further enrich the Saxons. Only one other Welshman escaped with his life, and that was Eidol of Gloucester who managed to get hold of a club and kill a number of Saxons before escaping. After this massacre, called the 'Betrayal of the Long Knives' by the Welsh, the Saxons compelled Gwrtheyrn to give them all the lands of Essex, Sussex and Middlesex.

The Betrayal of the Long Knives

Not enough's been told in our tales
Recounting the stories of Wales;
Not enough from those archives
Of the Betrayal of the Long Knives.

Eyes of Lloer, eyes of Llugwy,
Searching eyes of all who can see,
Seeking land across river to thrive
Came the Betrayal of the Long Knives.

Porth Dinllaen, Porth-gain, Porth Neigwl:
Gateways of memory and thought also;
Feeding lust and dirt of their lives
Came the Betrayal of the Long Knives.

Glyn-nedd, Glyncorrwg, Glyn y Groes:
Each glen with a melodious voice;
Ready to capture songs like their wives
Came the Betrayal of the Long Knives.

Ynys Dewi and Ynys Gwylan
Both with the warmth of Avalon;
Taken with greed in their eyes
Came the Betrayal of the Long Knives.

Hear the song of the river Tywi,
Dwyfor, Ebwy, Clwyd and Teifi;
Every river's song will survive
To tell of the Betrayal of the Long Knives.

The Land of Heledd and Cynddylan Wyn

Like many towns near the border between England and Wales, Shrewsbury is a lovely town to visit. It has a castle and an old abbey, and traces of its long and interesting history are very much in evidence. While walking around its museums and reading snippets of stories on information boards and in local history books, we learn that the Romans lived nearby, that the Saxons established the town and that the Normans made it their military base from which to invade Wales. But there is no mention that this area was once part of the land of the Welsh.

If we turn to early Welsh poetry, we get a different story. The Severn river rises in the mountains of mid-Wales, flows eastwards – via Shrewsbury – and then turns south. Until the seventh and eighth centuries all these lands were once Welsh territory: place names were Welsh, and it was the language of everyone, from peasants to princes. Certain early poems take us back to various historic periods and to different parts of Britain – all these lands were formerly part of a territory where Welsh was spoken, before the Saxon, English-speaking, occupation.

In a cycle of poems which are known as

'Heledd's Song' (*Canu Heledd*) we get the family history of Cynddylan Wyn. He was king of Old Powys in the seventh century, and his court was at Pengwern (by tradition, where Shrewsbury castle now stands). Heledd, sister of Cynddylan, is the narrator in the poems and we feel the weight of her loss and heartbreak. According to the poems, Cynddylan was fighting the men of England and was slain in battle defending Old Powys – now the Shropshire plain. He was buried at *Eglwysau Basa*. This place can be seen on the map today as Baschurch.

Many of the warriors were killed; the Saxons

Where is Pengwern tonight?

Tears of the river Severn on the meadow;
Place name in Welsh found on a scroll,
But Heledd will not return at all.

The banquet hall with silent, white boards;
Once lively soldiers' graves at the ford
And a longing that rises up loud.

Suddenly the thatched roof caught fire;
They slept so long as they were tired;
Their light rapidly expired.

A crowd in town about their day
And nobody wants to take a journey
Into the ancient poem on their way.

Water from hills flows under bridges,
Alder leaves fly towards the edges,
Pathways wind between the hedges.

Although there's snow on the horizon
And the fortress on the hill's broken down,
Under these streets lies Pengwern.

burned down Pengwern court, and laid waste to the countryside, farms and towns in the vicinity too. It was the end for the Welsh of Old Powys. The families fled to the mountains of Wales, following the course of the Severn to safer territory.

Welsh poetry confronts the losses and devastation following the warring. Nothing of this history is found up on walls or in guidebooks in Shrewsbury today, and yet – because we know about the Welsh poems – it is all still there, hidden below the surface. The odd street and business still bears the name 'Pengwern' to this day!

Offa's Dyke

Offa was king of the Saxons between 757 and 796 – the strongest of their kings up to that point. Although he did attack Wales and kill, raid and burn parts of it, he decided to concentrate on getting all quarters of England under his influence. To do that, he had to abandon his attacks on the Welsh and aim to contain them to prevent their retaliation against England. He decided to mark a boundary between the two countries and to prohibit anyone from crossing it.

The way he created the border was to build a dyke and dig a deep ditch; this is Offa's Dyke. The Dyke was more than two metres high in places, and the ditch – on the Welsh side – was two metres deep. The embankment was topped with a wooden fence. This border stretched 150 miles (240 kilometres) from Prestatyn in the north-east to Chepstow in the south-east, an immense feat for the eighth century. It was the largest construction in Europe until the canals of the early Industrial Revolution. It would have meant an immense army of workers. Its impression on the land is such that the remains of the Dyke can be seen from space.

The boundary between England (*Lloegr*) and Wales (*Cymru*) today is pretty similar to what it was 1,300 years ago, apart from lands reclaimed by the Welsh under Owain Gwynedd, which extended the boundary to Deeside. A long-distance footpath follows Offa's Dyke today; every year thousands walk it.

It persists deeper than the surface of the land too: in Welsh 'people from this side of Offa's Dyke' or 'people from the other side of the Dyke' are still referred to. The Dyke has heightened the differences between those of Celtic descent who live in the hills to the west and the Saxons living on the plains to the east.

In Offa's day, Welsh people who ventured across the Dyke were punished – it was said that it was not unusual for the Saxons to cut off the ears of any Welshman caught east of Offa's Dyke. An armed Welshman would have his hand cut off. And the fate of an Englishman caught on the western side wasn't pleasant either. It's believed that the Saxons kept lookouts here and there, using the height of the Dyke to keep an eye on the Welsh.

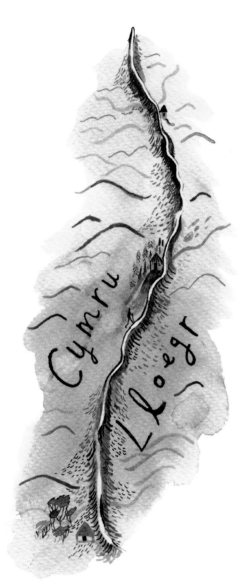

Egbert on Offa's Dyke

It is I, Egbert, the one who's spying,
Often through daytime and with the owl;
The wooden fence on the ridge shielding.

Spear in my hand – seven feet of ash,
Its iron front bright in the sun;
Here on the Dyke, swivelling around.

On guard and always peering;
Reporting any threat I detect;
Seeking out strangers my intention.

On the other side, fog on the mountain,
Tracks of mud and floodplains;
People who have no religion.

On the other side, crags and thorns,
Soil full of stones, infertile ground;
Rugged country with no civilisation.

They are nothing like us
With our lush pastures, cattle grazing,
Wheat in furrows, orchards flourishing.

They're so silent now – the rogues!
I can't understand the words they weave,
It is I, Egbert, watching for thieves.

The Norsemen!

There are many names for them – Norsemen, Danes, Vikings, Black Pagans. But all of these names produced the same shudder of fear and terror around the coast of Wales in the ninth and tenth centuries.

Norway, southern Sweden and Denmark were the homelands of the Norsemen and they were able sailors and adventurous people. The Norse hordes came in longboats that held about thirty soldiers and strong rowers, to pillage, burn and murder throughout northern Europe. They even established settlements on some Scottish islands, in northern England, and in Dublin. From there they could reach Wales and strike fear and terror into the coastal dwellers.

In 855 the Danes in Ireland sailed a flotilla of warships towards Wales. But Rhodri Mawr (Rhodri 'the great'), king of the Welsh at the time, had gathered an army to defend the country. Horm, leader of the Norsemen, was killed in battle on marshland near today's Llandudno, so ensuring Wales' safety.

But the Welsh continued to be tormented by these longships and their warlike sailors for years after this, and some place names in Wales are derived from the language of the Norsemen: Anglesey, Bardsey and Swansea (Ynys Môn, Ynys Enlli and Abertawe, in Welsh).

Tonight

F
U
M
I
N
G
tonight the wind
and waves rise and pound
the beach over and over
as if the rock
were Rhodri's shield
in days of old

F
I
N
E
tonight in my sleep
without fear of flames
or the blades of Danes
in the wild
foam's
fuming.

(The shape and content of this poem are based on the pattern of a poem composed by an Irish monk in the margin of a page of parchment during the age of the Horsemen.)

Gruffudd ap Cynan

Gruffudd ap Cynan was born and raised in Dublin – his mother was the princess there. But his father Cynan was king of Gwynedd and when the boy grew up he raised an army to reclaim the land of his fathers. Winning and losing was the story for years – repeatedly defeated by his enemies, he would flee to Ireland for asylum. The Normans were the thorn in his side: from their stronghold in Chester they would drive large armies into north Wales, and rapidly build castles to steal and control the land. Hugh Lupus was the Earl of Chester – nicknamed 'Hugh the Wolf' because of his character.

Gruffudd flourished for a while, and became a strong king in Gwynedd. He was invited to a peace conference at Rhug, near Corwen, to negotiate with Hugh the Wolf and the other Normans. But it was all a trap; Gruffudd's peaceful convoy was attacked. All his troops had their thumbs cut off and Gruffudd was thrown into the worst cell in Chester castle. He was dragged through the streets and put in the stocks near the Cross in front of the church every market day, so that the city crowds could mock him and pelt him with filth.

After the 16 years of Gruffudd's captivity – 16 years of suffering under the Normans in north Wales – an Edeyrnion man, Cynwrig Hir

(Cynwrig '*the tall*'), and his comrades seized Gruffudd from the stocks one day, whisked him past the sentries at the gates and the bridge, and over the Dee river back to Wales.

On his recuperation, Gruffudd led the Welsh in burning down every Norman castle in Gwynedd in 1094.

When we visit the city of Chester these days, it's worth pausing from our shopping to take a walk around the cathedral precincts to remember one of the kings of Wales who was maltreated here. Then, turn towards the river to see the old bridge over the Dee – a wooden bridge in Gruffudd's day, of course. A nearby plaque shows a historical scene: one of the many armies leaving Chester to attack north Wales. There's a picture of the bridge there too, with the city wall and round towers on the riverbank, and a fortified gatehouse standing in the current. These were necessary, according to the inscription, in order to protect the city from 'the marauding Welsh'!

Gruffudd in Chester prison

It's summer and sun pummels at my eyes
As I'm hauled from the stocks to the pit,
Crows at my feet pecking at waste
And all the market laughing at my cost.

The wolf's in his castle, in church his God,
There's harsh haggling over land and gold;
I'll dispatch a small and gentle dove
Over to the sea and mountains I love.

It's autumn, yellow leaves are whirling,
Someone's cursing the Welsh and their nation,
Seagulls squabble over the guts of a herring
Under the bell tower's stained glass window.

It's winter in the square, snow from the east,
The city's beggars scrabble over scraps,
Sometimes bitter buckets are spilled
From the taverns warm broth and smoke.

When spring comes it's the season's fair;
Welsh accents from the stalls so near,
In gardens the monks fertilise their land,
The warmth of manure on their hands.

The wolf's in his castle, in church his God,
There's harsh haggling over land and gold;
I'll dispatch a small and gentle dove
Over to the sea and mountains I love.

It's late and the crowd pushes through streets
Over the south bridge, sacks on their backs,
Where the Dee's water and willows sing
Of a journey home, of freedom.

Gwenllïan, daughter of Gruffudd

Gwenllïan was the youngest daughter of Gruffudd ap Cynan, prince of Gwynedd. She was born at court in Aberffraw, Anglesey in 1097 during her father's wars to rid north Wales of the Normans. She was the youngest of eight and extraordinarily beautiful, it seems.

Gruffudd ap Rhys, Prince of Deheubarth (south-western Wales), came to meet with Gruffudd ap Cynan in 1113 to discuss joint raids against the Normans. But he fell in love with the young princess. They eloped to live in Dinefwr castle and had eight children.

They had a troubled life: raising children while trying to keep Deheubarth free of the grip of ever-increasing numbers of Normans attacking the coast, stealing land and erecting castles to protect their gains. Gruffudd, Gwenllïan and the Welsh court had to leave Dinefwr castle and live in the wooded valleys, carrying out guerrilla attacks on the Normans before melting back into the safety of the countryside.

In 1136, the Welsh rose up in revolt against the Normans across large parts of the country. Hywel ap Maredudd, Lord of Brycheiniog (Brecon), led his army against the Normans of the Gower and vanquished them at the Battle of Garn Goch. Gruffudd and Gwenllïan were inspired by this victory and Gruffudd travelled to Anglesey to call on Gruffudd ap Cynan's support for a national uprising.

While Gruffudd was in the north, a message came saying Maurice de Londres, a Norman, had landed at Kidwelly and he and his army were travelling up the Gwendraeth valley to attack the Welsh.

There was no time to wait for Gruffudd to return from the north. Gwenllïan mustered her army and led them down the valley. She was used to fighting alongside her husband. She had her sons with her: Morgan was twenty, Maelgwn eighteen. As they passed through Welsh villages, farmers and workers joined their army, brandishing agricultural implements on their way to the battlefield.

The two armies met on level ground near the river, north of Kidwelly castle. The Norman army was large and better equipped. The Welsh lost the day. Gwenllïan was captured and beheaded by the Normans. Morgan was killed in battle and Maelgwn was executed alongside his mother.

Despite Gwenllïan's defeat, her courage served to inspire the Welsh. For centuries thereafter, the Welsh went into battle against the Normans with the cry 'Gwenllïan's Revenge!' Iorwerth ab Owain led the Welshmen of Gwent against the Norman Richard Fitz Gilbert de Clare and killed him. Gruffudd returned from Gwynedd with Owain

and Cadwaladr – Gwenllïan's brothers – and their armies, and they defeated the Normans in a series of battles in Ceredigion and Carmarthenshire.

'Maes Gwenllïan' ('*Gwenllïan's field*') is the name of a farm near Kidwelly castle to this day. She was the only Welsh princess to lead an army against the Normans and her rebellion is comparable to Buddug's (*Boudicca's*) against the Romans.

Gwenllïan on the battlefield

When the Normans came with stamping oppression
And stealing and murder were their intentions,
To take Cymru by violence, to destroy
Every household; man, woman, girl, boy.

  She was the waterfall, wind in her hair,
  She was holly's barbs laid bare,
  She was the oak shadowing the valley,
  She was thorn in flesh of the enemy.

When there was no flag, army or weapons
To raise up in an insurrection
And the Normans came like waves from sea
Threatening to engulf all of Tywi,

When its sons with swords in their hands
Declared they were brave, would save the land,
How could she keep them from battlefield
When her country cried out with need?

  She was the waterfall, wind in her hair,
  She was holly's barbs laid bare,
  She was the oak shadowing the valley,
  She was thorn in flesh of the enemy.

Should you come to this dale between wood and river,
The name of the place is the Field of Massacre,
There's sun on the dew and birds who sing,
It is Gwenllïan they are remembering.

Ifor Bach

In 1158, the Norman William Fitz Robert decided he wanted more land. He lived securely with one hundred of his soldiers in a tower of Cardiff castle, built on top of a motte (a high mound of earth). He sent his soldiers to the court of a Welshman, Morgan ab Owain, Lord of Caerleon and Gwynllwg. Morgan was killed and his property and lands seized by the Normans. Shortly after that, William Fitz Robert sent a strong army to Senghenydd on a similar mission. Ifor ap Meurig – known as 'Ifor Bach' ('*little Ifor*') because of his size – was the Lord Senghenydd and although the Normans captured a large part of his estate, he and his men eluded them.

In Cardiff castle the Norman felt safe and strong. But one night, Ifor Bach and his men taught him a lesson. They stealthily placed long ladders against the castle walls. Ifor was the first over the battlements; they searched the tower in darkness and found William Fitz Robert's bedroom. They tied up the Norman and his wife and carried them off, along with their baby son, to the mountain forests. Ifor refused to release them until the stolen lands – and a little more! – were returned to the Welsh of Senghenydd. After that, the Normans did not feel so safe in their castle strongholds.

Many of today's Cardiff Welsh enjoy contemporary Welsh entertainment at a nightclub called Clwb Ifor Bach, which is located right opposite the Cardiff castle walls that the little Senghenydd hero climbed nearly nine hundred years ago!

Capture of the Earl's castle

An earthen mound in Cardiff castle
Once surrounded by walls and a tower;
There, one night, with his Countess and son
One man was sleeping sound.

He was a Norman, William Fitz Robert,
Whose name spelt terror throughout,
With his army, weapons and fort
Nobody was his foe for long.

He slept peacefully that night
With a hundred soldiers or more in the tower,
No doubt chuckling as he dreamt
Of the petty Welshmen quaking with fear.

Very next day he sent to Senghenydd
His fiercest and strongest battalions
To capture land from Ifor Bach,
An easy task for his men.

While the Normans laughed about victory
Men approached through woods stealthily
Carrying hidden ladders, ropes and hooks,
To the base of the castle walls.

Ifor ap Meurig, such a small man,
Yet with the heart of a giant,
Was first to climb up like a squirrel
And he searched floor after floor.

He kidnapped Fitz Robert, wife and only son,
Brought them to Senghenydd woods,
Keeping them captive till they relented
And returned the land they'd stolen.

An earthen mound in Cardiff Castle
Surrounded by walls and a tower,
Yet stronger than stones and all the Normans
Were Ifor ap Meurig and his followers.

The Deceitful King

In 1158, after bloody campaigns to capture lands in Ireland, the English King Henry II turned his sights on Deheubarth. Owain Gwynedd's grip on the north of the country was unassailable and the Lord Rhys had a strong grip on the Tywi valley, Pembrokeshire and Ceredigion, building a series of stone castles. Henry invited the Lord Rhys of Deheubarth and his retinue to peace talks at his court in Worcester, promising him security and reasonable terms. When the Welsh reached the city, they were all thrown into the castle's prison. Henry sent one of his most trusted soldiers to Rhys' lands – in particular to Dinefwr castle – to see how fruitful the land was and how rich its inhabitants, to assess whether it would be worth the cost of going to war to capture it. Henry's spies forced Gwyddan – the foremost churchman of the Cantref Mawr – to guide them around the area. Fortunately, this man of the cloth believed the Welsh proverb: 'Deceiving a deceiver is no deception'!

Gwyddan the Fox

Thief of the first order, Henry II,
Once eyed up Carmarthen and Cardigan.

'What kind of place is this?'
There was no 'Visit Wales'
And no Google then,
There was no choice
But to spy on them.

Lord Rhys was prince of the Welsh:
Rhys with his bold fortresses.
'Come, let's talk peace,' said the cunning king,
Raising the white banner of England
But throwing him into prison.

Then he commanded a soldier
To bring him information on Dinefwr –
How powerful the castle,
How much French wine in the cellar?
He could then decide
If it was worth invading.

The soldier claimed only one man under God,
Namely Gwyddan the Good, could lead the way.

'This is the road to take,' explained Gwyddan,
Who now became fox-like,
Fouling his sandals in muddy pools
And scrambling over rocky slopes.

'This is the easiest path, the best one,'
He insisted, a fox on the run.

'I've a terrible thirst!' moaned the soldier.
'Don't worry, that's simple to quench,'
Answered Gwyddan, bending to sip
Dirty water from a ditch – 'Ah, like wine!
Mud gives body to this drink!
Its taste stays long on the tongue.'

'It's time to eat!' groaned the king's man.
'No problem at all, the strangest taste
In the world is around us.' Gwyddan began
To chew on grass, chomp at its roots,
Praising every green stalk:
'Here in Wales we eat for health.'

'When do we reach the castle?'
'But we're there already,' replied Gwyddan.
'The rocks are its walls, branches its roof,
Beds the ferns you see growing.
Why not sleep after the feasting?'
Gwyddan lay down, fox in its den.

The soldier fled, reporting to the King
That savages lived in Carmarthen
And there was no point taking a land
Where folk ate grass and drank mud.

Rhys was set free and in Dinefwr
A great banquet welcomed him home.

The Lord Rhys
and the First Eisteddfod

The National Eisteddfod is a festival that celebrates all aspects of Welsh life and being Welsh, and it also provides a platform to address current affairs. Walking around the colourful *Maes* (the Eisteddfod field) is also great fun.

According to an old history of the Welsh Princes, the first eisteddfod was held at Cardigan (*Aberteifi*) castle at Christmas, 1176. It was publicised in every court in Wales a year in advance and a chair was presented to the best poet, and another to the best musician from among the harpists, pipers and *crwth* players who attended.

The Lord Rhys, owner of the castle, organised the festival. But it was more than a competition: it was a celebration of the Welsh recapturing Ceredigion from the Normans' grip.

That campaign began in 1136 with a huge victory over the Normans by Owain Gwynedd and Gruffudd, father of the Lord Rhys, at the Battle of Crug Mawr, two miles north of Cardigan. The Normans were driven into the Teifi river – the town's bridge broke under the weight of those fleeing; drowned bodies blocked the river's flow.

Stones by the river

A circle of stones
Near the river's sound,
Warmed by the sun
Washed by the rain.

A protected place
And one of meeting,
Jangle of swords
Raised for the Eisteddfod.

Stones standing firm
And one in togetherness,
Holding the light,
Outlasting the storms.

The best of musicians
And magicians with words,
The Chair is ready
And everyone's listening.

Stones in circles
Count out the years,
The holding of festivals
And tales of the Maes.

Rhys ap Gruffudd succeeded his father as Prince of Deheubarth, capturing and razing a number of Norman castles in south-west Wales. In 1165, Cardigan castle came into his possession, but instead of destroying it, Rhys moved his main court there and in 1171 began to construct a stone castle on top of the original Norman motte and bailey. This was the first stone castle built by a Welshman. By then he had the upper hand over his enemies, and by so doing he was formally acknowledged as the Lord of Deheubarth – the Lord Rhys.

At Christmas 1176, the Lord Rhys held an eisteddfod in his new castle. The stone castle became home to Welsh culture. As well as poetry and song, the success of the Welsh on the battlefield was celebrated at this first eisteddfod. More recently, there has been a tradition of constructing a stone circle for ceremonies held by the Gorsedd (the *Gorsedd of the Bards*) in towns the National Eisteddfod visits.

The Lord Rhys and Nevern Castle

The remains of Nevern castle can be seen a little uphill from the old church in the village. The Lord Rhys captured the castle from the Norman, Fitzmartin, in 1191 and it was one of their strongholds in Deheubarth before the Welsh wrecked and abandoned it.

The valley of the Nyfer river is narrow and wooded and the water flows darkly on its way to the sea near Newport. When it rains, the river rises and floods quickly, red with mud. Then, when the storm abates, it recedes and is clear once again.

We camped beside the river during the Urdd Eisteddfod in Pembroke in 2013 and we saw these abrupt changes in the nature of the river. Another sign of the weather was the two hundred or more swallows darting above the river at the campsite in the evenings. When the swallows flew high it meant good weather; but if they were swooping low over the water to catch insects – rain.

Fair weather and storm was also the story of the Welsh in the Norman period, and this Eisteddfod certainly brought the Lord Rhys to mind.

Swallows of the river Nevern

White feather of a dying cloud
Today lies still on the oak,
Sea mist hides the mountain
And hillsides in silence.

Incessant rain and the peat
Have reddened the flowing river,
As blue swallows dart
In the thick air above.

Another shower cannot kill
The passion which stays within,
We go to the field, there's a need
To raise Preseli's walls again.

Colours of May on every branch
Attract the distinctive rays
With their quiet coming
From the white horizon.

Late and air's full of chattering,
Song of river quartz-sparkling
And the spinning of blue birds
High above riverside oaks.

Gruffudd in the Tower

If you go to London, you may get a chance to visit one of the strongest castles in the world: the Tower of London. William the Conqueror, the Norman who defeated the English at Hastings in 1066, fortified it. William was determined to impress his authority and military strength on the people of the capital, and built the tall Tower on the bank of the Thames.

The Tower had a dual purpose from the outset: to create a secure home for the royal family of England, as well as a prison to house those enemies that posed the greatest threat to the kingdom. A number were killed there. The Traitors' Gate is built into the protective walls, leading straight into the strongest prison in England in those days. The kings of France and Scotland were imprisoned in the Tower, and Welsh princes and princesses were held too.

When an English king was holding peace talks with Welsh princes, as a rule he claimed the sons of the most important families as a hostage. If, in the king's view, any of the terms of the peace had been broken, the hostages would suffer. Henry II blinded the sons of Owain Gwynedd with hot irons, for example.

Llywelyn Fawr (Llywelyn '*the great*') won several victories over the English but, while negotiating peace with King John, he often had to give his son, Gruffudd, as such a hostage. Dafydd succeeded Llywelyn in 1240. Following a war a year later, Dafydd transferred his brother Gruffudd as a hostage to Henry III. Gruffudd was taken from his home in Llŷn to face imprisonment in the Tower.

Gruffudd's wife paid a ransom to release her husband, giving her two youngest sons as hostages as well. But Henry broke his word: he kept Gruffudd in the Tower to be used as a bargaining chip against the Welsh.

After three years in the Tower, Gruffudd had had enough. He decided to escape. He made a rope of sheets and blankets. There was a window in his room – a window on the south side of the Tower, on the top floor. He anchored his makeshift rope and climbed out of the window on the last night of February, 1244.

But years in prison had made Gruffudd ungainly. He looked upriver for the last time – if he followed his gaze, he would travel west towards the hills of Wales, the sound of Welsh and the company of friends. Stepping out, the sheets and blankets took his full weight, high above the ground. He began to let himself down, hand over hand, but one of the knots gave way. Gruffudd fell all the way down. Next day – Saint David's Day – Gruffudd's dead body was found at the foot of the White Tower. The window of his room was bricked up after that – but it's still possible to see it in the south wall. Looking at the south face of the White Tower, count the windows on the top floor on the left side. The seventh and eighth from the left are bricked up – this was Gruffudd's room.

In 1248, monks from Strata Florida arranged for his body to be returned to Wales and he was buried with his father in Aberconwy Abbey.

Leaving prison

Under the White Tower
The hill is sloping
And walls lead to the river;
On a night like this
The moon so round
It's easy to imagine
Being carried by water
To dream of Nefyn
And the valley of Nanhoron.

Through the south window
The sun is setting,
That's the path to follow
And I picture myself
In my home of Llŷn,
Children full of stories and fun;
There are men on the beach
Bows at the ready,
Blacksmith with the spark of iron.

Up three windows, three floors,
Above the large yard;
Tall as ten tall men standing,
Six white sheets will drop
Each tied with a heavy knot;
Halfway between heaven and earth,
Six thick blankets
Finish off the rope
Dangling all the way to the ground.

Every day Gruffudd sits
And dreams of freedom
Tearing bedclothes with his hands;
Stretching them long
Down to the ground;
One night of opportunity
Tying one end firmly,
Sneaking the rest through an opening,
Fleeing once and for all.

What would you see then
With the coming of dawn
But two of the look-outs yelling,
Two stable boys rushing over
To see what was going on
And Gruffudd lying there
In a lake of his blood,
The rope's snake broken.

In Nefyn in Llŷn
At that very time
His people heard the story,
How one man's longing
Outweighed a mighty tower
And king who'd overpower,
How he made a rope
His means of escape
At dawn on the day of St David.

The Battle of the Menai Strait

Dafydd ap Gruffudd ignited the flame of independence in Wales in the spring of 1282 by attacking the English castle at Hawarden, Flintshire. Dafydd was joined by his brother, Llywelyn ein Llyw Olaf (Llywelyn *our last leader*); their hope was to free the country from the hold of the Normans. Llywelyn already had many successes against them and had unified the whole of Wales under his authority. Even the English crown acknowledged that Llywelyn had retained the right to bear the title 'Prince of Wales'. But in the autumn of that year Edward I, the English king, brought a huge army to Anglesey to burn all the crops.

'Môn, Mam Cymru' ('*Anglesey, mother of Wales*') is the old saying, and all of Gwynedd depended on Anglesey's crops for food through the winter. From the shore at Felinheli a strange sight was seen: Edward's army tying boats together opposite Moel y Don to create a floating 'bridge' across the Strait.

By the sixth of November, the bridge was complete. Edward's intention was to cross using a wooden walkway laid across the boats, defeat the Welsh, and occupy all Snowdonia. When the tide was at its lowest ebb, his master plan started. His horsemen crossed first, in single file, followed by the foot soldiers.

All the while, the Welsh had seen his plans taking shape from their positions along the Anglesey shore. Rather than attacking the first across, the Welsh held off patiently. They let the cavalry cross and form a rank at the water's edge. They waited until about half of the infantry were on the bridge, then released a hail of arrows from the trees and steep cliffs above the beach. The Welsh had the advantage of the terrain and by now the tide had turned and was rising fast.

Horses were useless in a battle among trees and rocks and the Welsh attacked yet more fiercely as some riders tried to flee, back from Anglesey. Chaos enveloped the English and Normans: half the army trying to cross, the other half trying to cross back, and all the while the water rising. Most of Edward's army were slaughtered or drowned, and the Welsh celebrated a great victory at Moel y Don.

Moel y Don

White winter's biting at Moel y Don
Yet there's some comfort within:
The grain is stored in barns
And the mill-wheel's turning;
A kind of peace at Moel y Don.

Smoke like a black ghost over Moel y Don,
Each store, house and chest, stack of corn
Kept away from enemy flames;
And all the land of Llywelyn
Feared starvation's pain at Moel y Don.

A bridge raised by boats on Moel y Don,
Stout ropes holding planks firm;
An army of knights waiting
By the river and menacing,
The banks themselves tremble at Moel y Don.

Patience the word at Moel y Don
Each bow and spear in expectation;
When the tides are rising
Arrows of fire come speeding
From Welshmen in woods, upon Moel y Don.

Menai reddened with blood by Moel y Don
As the Normans are retreating;
Pride was high as the sun
Because the rocky shields of Arfon
Won the day at Moel y Don.

Burying Llywelyn ein Llyw Olaf

The Welsh princes endowed many abbeys in their provinces by giving land and money, buildings, mills and fishing rights. The 'white monks' were their favourite order and a number of princes are buried in the abbeys of Aberconwy, Valle Crucis, Strata Florida, Whitland (Hendy-gwyn ar Daf) and Talley (Talyllychau). In Radnorshire stand the ruins of Abbey Cwmhir, where the remains of Llywelyn ein Llyw Olaf were buried. Llywelyn was killed in a skirmish at a battle at Cilmeri in mid-Wales on 11 December, 1282. The prince's head was cut off and put on a spike at the Tower of London. How glad the English king was to be rid of this Welshman, so long a thorn in his side! Wales was plunged into deep sadness, but some of Llywelyn's followers secretly moved his body so it could be buried in sanctified ground in a remote valley at Abbey Cwm-hir.

Today, an extraordinary peacefulness pervades Cwm-hir. Ruins and a memorial slab are all you can see; yet something draws us to this place, to remember the past. Something remains, despite so much having been lost.

Abbey Cwm-hir

It's autumn with leaves littering,
Bottoms of jeans damp with dew
From clumsily slipping downslope
Just to see these stones.

In the valley, all morning long,
A lazy haze across the land;
The white walls fill our eyes
When we go to see these stones.

Ignoring us on our foolish ways
The red ponies intently graze,
They raise heads to look around
When we go to see these stones.

The sunlight points to words
Written on a single slate plaque
By monks who once lived by the lake,
When we go to see these stones.

Just a story from days of old
And another winter wind,
The creaking of a closing gate
When we go to see these stones.

The Children of the Princes

In the eyes of Edward I, occupying Wales and destroying the houses and castles of her princes was not enough. It was necessary to destroy her future. And the future is always in the hands of the children.

Llywelyn ap Gruffudd had one daughter: Gwenllïan. She was born on 12 June, 1282, six months before her father's murder in an ambush at Cilmeri on 11 December. Eleanor, Gwenllïan's mother, died soon after giving birth. Gwenllïan was the only child, and at a few months old she was an orphan at court in Abergwyn-gregyn, near Bangor.

Dafydd, Llywelyn's brother, received the title 'Prince of Wales' after Cilmeri. Edward's huge mercenary armies now rampaged through every valley in Snowdonia, killing and destroying. The Welsh castles fell one by one – Dolwyddelan, Cricieth, Y Bere, Dolbadarn. In June 1283, Dafydd ap Gruffudd was caught, and in the October he was dragged behind a horse through the streets of Shrewsbury to a grisly death.

Dafydd's wife, Elizabeth, and their two sons and seven daughters were imprisoned in Rhuddlan castle. Owain (7 years old) and Llywelyn (4) were the names of his sons, but we only have the name of one of the girls: Gwladus.

Although there were only children left after the two princes' deaths, Edward still saw them as a threat. He knew very well that in their hearts the Welsh wanted to remain independent from the Normans' clutch. He knew that these children would grow up to threaten his armies again, with all Wales ready to fight for the country's release.

In November 1283 Edward sent Dafydd's daughters to Sixhills Priory in Lincolnshire and Gwenllïan to Sempringham Priory in the same county. This is on the opposite side of the country to Gwynedd – it would have taken days to reach in those days. The girls were kept captive and forced to become nuns – and nuns cannot marry or have children. They were in closed orders, and so not allowed to speak, and it is possible that the sisters were separated, unable even to be company or comfort to

Only children

Gwenllïan of Abergwyn-gregyn;
Gwladus and Owain and Llywelyn.

Children without favours or fun
And nobody to care for them.

Children with no room to roam,
Only walls of wood and stone.

Children who never get answers,
Only the turning locks of masters.

Children in the enemy's hands;
Children growing up without friends.

Children who cry in the night,
A strange game of Hide 'n' Fright.

Gwenllïan of Abergwyn-gregyn;
Gwladus and Owain and Llywelyn.

each other. Gwladus died in the nunnery in 1336, having spent 53 years there. A year later, her cousin Gwenllïan died in the Sempringham nunnery.

Owain and Llywelyn, the sons of Dafydd, were taken to a dungeon in the prison of Bristol castle in July 1283. They were held there for the rest of their days. Llywelyn died as a boy of nine. In 1312, the unfortunate Owain – confined in a wooden cage in his prison cell – wrote a letter to King Edward asking if he could be released for a while every day to go out and play within the castle walls. By then Owain was 36 years old. He was still there at 49. There is no record of his death.

After 1282

Although Llywelyn's killing in Cilmeri in 1282 was a heavy blow to the Welsh leadership, the Normans didn't have it all their own way in our country. Several rebellions in Wales between 1282 and 1316 saw a number of their new castles fall into the hands of the Welsh, who were already fed up of the oppressive Norman regime.

The first leader to rebel against the invaders was Rhys ap Maredudd of Deheubarth. The Lord Rhys was his great-grandfather and Dinefwr castle, near Llandeilo – one of the three foremost royal courts of Wales – was Rhys ap Maredudd's centre as well.

Edward I forced Rhys to surrender Dinefwr castle by claiming that he was now the true owner of Deheubarth. Rhys moved from Dinefwr to Dryslwyn castle, lower down the Tywi valley. But in 1283 Edward insisted Dryslwyn belonged to him too. This led to a quarrel and the quarrel escalated into rebellion in 1287.

The Welsh of the Tywi valley rose with Rhys to reoccupy their traditional lands. Rhys and his followers captured the castles of Dinefwr, Carreg Cennen, and Newcastle Emlyn (*Castell Newydd Emlyn*). He was cornered in Newcastle Emlyn castle in 1288, which fell to the English king's men after a ten-day siege.

But Rhys had already escaped! He lived as an outlaw in the countryside of Carmarthenshire for three years.

The king and the hills

'Surrender, stubborn Welshman,
Surrender, Rhys!'
Says the king.
'Here is my court,
Here my walls and moat,
Here my hall to nightly banquet,
Here my fort with silver hidden,
Just because I am a Norman.'

'Stand firm, brave Welshman,
Stand firm, Rhys!'
Say the hills.
'Here is your court,
Here the stream sings in your heart,
Here rocks keep enemies out,
Here the sun's your shining blade,
Just because you are a Welshman.'

'Surrender, Welshman!' says the king.
'A prison is waiting for you.'

'Stand firm, Welshman!' say the hills,
'This is the land that makes you.'

Edward I's Imprisonment in Conwy

After Llywelyn ap Gruffudd's murder at Cilmeri, many thought the end of the road had come, and that Wales would be engulfed by the king of England. Armies from Chester fanned out over north Wales, carving roads through the wild woods and starting work on new castles.

Edward did not believe that a single castle would be enough to ensure control over the Welsh. He took over existing castles at Rhuddlan, Denbigh and Cricieth and strengthened them. He built a chain of new castles – unlike anything in the world at that time – at Ruthin (*Rhuthun*), Flint, Conwy, Caernarfon, Harlech and Beaumaris. The cost was astronomical; it almost bankrupted the English crown. After this building programme, Wales has the highest density of castles in Europe.

But Edward wasn't content that the castles merely housed his troops. He wanted to change the language and the habits of the Welsh – he wanted to force them to abandon their own culture and legal system.

To achieve this he knew he would have to attract a lot of Normans and English to live in Wales; this he did by making them more powerful and influential than the Welsh. He built new towns for the settlers within fortified walls that extended from the castles, surrounding each town so it would be safe from any attack.

The Welsh people's land was sold cheaply to these strangers; the Welsh were not allowed to buy land or houses in the new fortified towns – the Welsh weren't even allowed to live in them. The English townsfolk were granted more rights to trade than the local Welsh, and this forced the Welsh to sell their products for whatever price was offered in the towns' markets. On top of that, heavy taxes were imposed on the Welsh to raise money for the king's castle-building and his new military regime. English law replaced the old Welsh laws of Hywel Dda (Hywel '*the good*') in these colonists' towns. Although the valleys beyond the walls remained Welsh in nature and hostile to the new regime, several of these new towns and castles were situated on the coast, so ships coming in from the sea could service them.

Conwy is a good example of Edward's scheme: the castle is immensely strong, with high towers and a large gatehouse, built on a rock beside the river. There are strong walls surrounding the town and a small harbour in the estuary. The whole set-up leaves one in no doubt that one powerful enemy has totally defeated the other.

But there is another side to the story of Conwy. In 1294, when the town was no more than ten years old, the Welsh rose in revolt against Edward's new castles and towns. New settlements all over Wales were attacked. Two English armies sent to quell the rebels were vanquished. Edward urgently sent another army to cross the Conwy river. Heavy rains swept in and the river burst its banks, preventing these reinforcements and supplies from crossing the estuary to relieve the king. Madog ap Llywelyn, the leader of the Welsh revolt, and his mountain armies surrounded the town. The battlements were too high for them to climb over, so they camped at every one of the gates leading into the town. The town was under siege: no one could move in or out.

Gradually, food became scarce. There were wells within the town but, after several weeks, food had run out completely, except for some pots of honey. The army was starving and weakened and even Edward himself was trapped, having returned to 'teach the Welsh a lesson'. Throughout this crisis this proud king and his men had only water and honey to sustain them. Unfortunately for the Welsh, the rain stopped, the flood receded and eventually the rest of his army could reach the town with more soldiers and food to lift the siege.

By this stage Edward I realised he had not really conquered the Welsh. Only the little bits of land within the walls and castles were his domain.

The king and his castle

November under the grey towers
And my army deadened by hunger;
Wind and rain raising the waves:
Our castle a prison in stormy weather.

I am weak after a long time
Watching this land fall from our fingers,
Only a taste of honey and water,
Men distraught as despair lingers.

Welshmen at the gates of the town,
No knowing where their arrows come from;
Bad news blown from Caernarfon,
Smoke rising and its walls knocked down.

Unable to escape through Penmaenmawr,
A shower of rocks came hurtling down;
Back to Conwy where we were trapped
As water filled the river from Snowdon.

I am here in this fine hall
With dry mouth and belly groaning;
Welshmen massed outside the walls
And the dark weather gathering.

The Detested Castles and Towns

The purpose of the new towns and castles was to keep the Welsh poor –slaves to all intents and purposes – on the unproductive land, while wealth and power were in the hands the settlers in the walled towns who claimed the country for their own: the colonists. The hope was that the Welsh would be too impoverished to fight for independence ever again.

But the Welsh hated the new towns and castles. In 1400 Owain Glyndŵr and his followers rebelled against this state of affairs, but the result was the creation of yet more English laws to penalise the Welsh.

The aim of these Penal Laws was to suppress both nation and language, and smother the flames of rebellion. This is clear from the clause outlawing poets. The authorities knew what effect poetry had on the Welsh – leaders and commoners alike. The poets would remind people of their history, their heroism, and keep alive the hope of freedom. Poets have always been great agitators, so it was essential to silence their voices. 'There shall be no rhymers in Wales,' stated the Penal Laws, but poets still sing and speak in Welsh.

You cannot rhyme

You cannot live in a town;
You cannot open a shop;
You cannot purchase land
Or rise above your station;
You hardly exist
And cannot raise your voice;
But worse than this, my child of bliss,
You cannot rhyme.

You can't wish the King of England
Be thrown into cawl
With the leeks to boil and boil
Until he tastes of brine:
Because you cannot rhyme.

You can't claim that Dafydd Gam *
Smells like the bloomers of his mam
And he's head to foot
Without a spine,
Because you cannot rhyme.

You can't say we'll raise the Dragon,
That caves will echo with our song
Rather than pay our taxes
To Kidwelly's barons of crime,
Because this indeed will rhyme.

* A relation of Owain, and his betrayer.

*You cannot insult Lord Grey ***
And call him a greedy pig
Who is better roasted on a spit
In a feast so fine,
Because you cannot rhyme.

You can't proclaim freedom will come,
How folk will rise up soon,
Nor try to raise the spirits
Of those who are feeling down,
Because you cannot rhyme.

But you'll whisper, under your breath, hand over mouth:
Owain, the candle flame, light in the mirror
And a dream of tomorrow's country
Because there's no rhyming there.

In the end, there is only poetry.

*** Baron of Ruthin town and castle, land-grabber and Owain's enemy.*

Owain, the Astute and Cunning Leader

Wales is a compact land, and Owain Glyndŵr had a small army compared with the wealth and might of the Anglo-Normans. But Owain had learned quite a bit about the old ways the Welsh had of overcoming size disadvantage. 'If you're not strong, be cunning', as the old saying goes.

He used the weather astutely. Sometimes, a small band of his troops would attack the enemy in the middle of a thunderstorm and so carry the day. On one occasion the Welsh faced an army twice its size on Hyddgen moor, above Machynlleth. Owain positioned his men with their backs to the west and waited until the sun was low and bright, just before sunset, then attacked quickly and fiercely on horseback. With the sun blinding the Normans, the Welsh were able to destroy them and win a sweeping victory.

He used the land of Wales to his advantage too. He always tried to claim the high ground so that his enemy would have to labour uphill in battle, and this also gave greater force and speed to his troops' attacks, as in the battle of Hyddgen. Woodlands, and narrow passes and valleys, were used for speedy attacks and retreats. He knew the direct pathways over the mountains and could be on the attack in north Wales at the start of the week and a few days later be down south.

With one thing and another, the word among the Norman and English armies was that this Owain was quite a magician: he could even control the weather! These foreign armies feared the magic of Glyndŵr.

The following tale illustrates Glyndŵr's cunning perfectly.

Owain and his companions were on a spying mission through south Wales, collecting information about the Normans and their castles and their troop numbers. They were unarmed and their dress and horses give the impression that they were strangers rather than Welshmen. They arrived at Coity castle in the Vale of Glamorgan and asked the constable of the castle, Sir Lawrence Berclos, if they could stay overnight. Glyndŵr asked in French: he could speak several languages, of course.

Owain and his 'servant' were made welcome and, having eaten a good meal, Owain entertained officials of the castle with numerous stories and anecdotes. They had such a good time that Sir Lawrence Berclos insisted they stay longer. The two Welshmen were there for three nights. This is the exchange between the generous Sir Lawrence and his guests:

'You're most welcome to stay another night. I have bands of soldiers combing the surrounding

countryside for that Owain Glyndŵr devil and his gang. I wouldn't be surprised if they're caught by tomorrow and you'll have the privilege of seeing that villain in irons, here in my castle.'

And Owain replied:

'See Owain here in Coity castle? That would give me great satisfaction, Sir Lawrence! I can't wait until morning to see that scoundrel in your custody.'

After three nights of playing cat and mouse like this, Owain decided to continue on his way. He had gleaned a lot of useful information about his enemies by speaking perfect French to the constable. Before riding through the gate, he turned to his host and shook his hand, saying,

'With my hand on heart, Sir Lawrence Berclos, I will never do you harm nor seek revenge on you for all the hateful things you've said about me. For it is I, Owain Glyndŵr, who shakes your hand and thanks you for the generous welcome you have given my companion and me. Good day to you.'

Sir Lawrence was struck dumb there and then and, so the story goes, he never said a word again.

Glyndŵr's last words in Coety castle

'Thanks for your warning, O splendid Berclos,
Your words are so wise;
They must heed your advice
To take care whilst wandering hills
Lest Glyndŵr's soft-brained followers
Happen upon our meeting-place.

'Thanks for the news, O faithful Berclos,
So pleasant to have your assurance
That two hundred brave Normans
Are searching the whole land like hounds
To capture Glyndŵr and his minions
And they are here to defend us.

'As your guest I'm grateful, O hospitable Berclos
For countless wines and banquets;
Within your steadfast stronghold,
Behind your huge battlements,
Honoured to be in civilized company;
Wonderful to be at your side.

'Thanks for your guidance, O decisive Berclos,
For the mysteries of your castle,
For zealously showing the secrets
In the pit of the prison tower,
Place to fling a warring Welshman;
Your purpose is very clear.

'I respectfully give thanks, O sagacious Berclos,
These my pledges to you:
When I, Glyndŵr, and my army
Swallow your castle like a pudding
We will treat you like a king
As you have been so gracious to me!'

The Pennal Letter

This letter – written in Latin from Owain Glyndŵr, Prince of Wales, to Charles VI, the king of France – is remarkable and extremely valuable. It is the closest we come to hearing Owain speaking to us across the centuries. It shows Owain's skill as leader of a new country, in discussion with other European leaders. The original parchment is in a Paris museum, but it was returned to Wales in 2000 for the 600th anniversary celebrations of the Glyndŵr rebellion.

The letter is dated 31 March, 1406 and was written at Pennal, between Machynlleth and Aberdyfi. Glyndŵr received a letter from Charles VI on 8 March asking for support in establishing the pope in Avignon, France. The French and Welsh were on good terms, with ambassadors maintaining close contact between the two leaders. French delegates attended Glyndŵr's parliaments, and in August 1405 France sent thousands of soldiers to fight alongside the Welsh. Afterwards, Owain called a parliament at Pennal to discuss his reply to the French king's request.

By supporting the French, Glyndŵr and his parliament show that they have bold and definite plans to ensure a prosperous and independent future for Wales. In the letter he says he wants to get rid of Henry, king of England – 'the intruder of the kingdom of England' as he is called – and he condemns 'the fury of the barbarous Saxons'.

We have to remember that England had just issued the Penal Laws, which prevented the Welsh from holding jobs and owning property in the colonists' towns, from defending themselves, and from using Welsh. They were treated as aliens their own country. We see in the Pennal Letter – and other letters Glyndŵr wrote – the Welsh wishing to unite and reclaim their traditional land, and to hold a parliament and be responsible for their own future. This is a vision for a new Wales, without the oppressive castles; with its own archbishopric at St David's; independent universities; Welsh as the language of the law; and courts and a parliament to express the voice of the people.

Most of this is expressed in the Pennal Letter, a historic document in which the Welsh nation recovers its self-respect and confidence in a bright future.

I see a land

I see a land, said the shepherd,
Without the fear of conquerors,
A place where all's a fair price
And peace the most common word.

I see a land, said the monk,
Where you can pray in Welsh to God,
Where children can venture forth
Educated, to sow the seeds of love.

I see a land, said the soldier,
With iron at its very heart,
Where valleys and vales are protected
From wolf and hawk, famine and flood.

I see a land, said the prince,
Where people are advised daily,
Where justice is vigorously applied
And everyone's views heard freely.

We see a land, the people declared,
Rising from Glyndŵr's parchment,
Letters across the centuries,
A dream of great equality.

The Skylark Retreats

After fifteen years of warfare, remnants of Owain Glyndŵr's army took refuge in the mountains and caves, but Owain was never caught.

Troops, spies and bounty killers were sent from England to corner or kill him, but all failed. A huge reward was offered for information about him, but he was never betrayed by his fellow countrymen. He refused to accept the terms of the English king and ignored an offered pardon from an alien crown. He lay low: first as an outlaw, and then he went into hiding. When he died and where he is buried are still unknown. His story turned into legend and his name kept the independent spirit of the Welsh alive.

When writing about this final phase, the words of the Welsh chronicler are heavy with significance: '1415: Owain went into hiding on Saint Matthew's Day in Harvest, and thereafter his hiding place was unknown. Very many said that he died; the seers maintain he did not.'

'*Brudwyr*' were prophetic poets, and they proclaimed that Owain would rise to lead his nation once again: 'Myn Duw, mi a wn y daw' (*'By God, I know he will come'*). For generations following the revolt, many Welsh people lived as outlaws rather than give in to the ways and laws of the English. No poet ever sang a poem in memory of Glyndŵr, and that speaks volumes. Folk stories insist that Owain's spirit is still alive in the land.

There is a verse – an ancient verse – which is still sung, titled 'Marwnad yr Ehedydd' ('*the*

skylark's elegy'). According to tradition, Glyndŵr or one of his lieutenants, still outlawed, is the 'skylark' in the song. The first verse is traditional but the rest is legend.

Praise the Lark

*I heard that the Lark
Had died on the mountainside
And keened as the man spoke,
As no more men with weapons
Could bring its body home.*

*Afterwards, the long yellow summer
Turned into a mist hanging
And no one inclined to take the day
With fresh wings, ignore the weather
And venture over the moorland.*

*I heard some whispering
That the nest had been destroyed
By a buzzard on the beacons
With all the darkness of death
In its claws and eyes.*

*There are look-outs on Plynlimon
Hunters in the woods of Glyn Cynon,
No free birds in Mawddwy,
Yet the same deer in Nant Conwy,
The same salmon in Glyndyfrdwy.*

*Yet some quiet little words,
No more than breeze through heather,
Told that one day a harpist would sing
Without a single syllable of English
And the Lark would rise again.*

Dafydd ap Siencyn

Dafydd ap Siencyn of Nant Conwy was a very adventurous man. He lived sometime between 1430 and 1495, the period after Owain Glyndŵr's war of independence. Almost every town in Wales was destroyed during that war; Owain and his army attacked the Anglo-Norman towns and castles, and the king's armies attacked Welsh towns and homes. Nant Conwy – the upper Conwy valley – was a hotbed of support for Glyndŵr. Two brothers, Rhys Gethin and Hywel Coetmor, came from this area and both were important generals in his army. An English army swept through the Conwy valley in 1403 and burned Llanrwst to the ground. The locals fled to the surrounding woods and hills, living as 'outlaws': living rough, outside the law, under the cover of the tree-clad hillsides. Although the war had ended, many Welsh people continued to live as outlaws until well after 1500, and were known as 'Children of Owain'.

Dafydd ap Siencyn was a 'child of Owain', and lived with a band of outlaws from Nant Conwy who supported him. They lived in a cave in the Carreg y Gwalch (*carreg*: rock; *gwalch*: hawk) cliff and from time to time a posse of soldiers would come from Conwy Castle to look for him. But Dafydd was an expert longbowman!

The Hawk's Crag

The Welsh were never ones for comfort,
Time of the wild deer there was Hawk in the wood.

His plume trailed green leaves of ash tree
And on the crag he was free.

His rocky castle rose over the meadow
Where no army would dare to go.

A glorious castle where friends were welcome;
A fatal fall for enemies who'd come.

A band of men lived in a cave at that time
And, like him, they lived in freedom.

Children of Glyndŵr's flame, some say. To those
Who lived in the big fortress they were rogues.

Dafydd ap Siencyn, with bow and arrow,
Refused to be caught, to kow-tow.

'Pay taxes to the English,' the officer spoke,
'I'd rather feast on deer,' replied the Hawk.

In the end, strong troops came marching
Into Llanrwst's streets and searching

For someone to lead through woods and rocks
To the mouth of the cave so black.

The town answered with shut doors. Every road
Was empty and nobody volunteered.

'Such Welsh!' said the angry Captain
'There's a rock where they are hiding –

'Just through the woods and over the river,
Capture and kill them, easiest thing ever.'

'But for now we must eat and it's better for sure
To satisfy hunger on the other side of the water.'

The soldiers all sat at the bottom of the glen
And took out a pie they'd brought with them,

Placed it on a rug and were ready …
But the mood of the day changed rapidly.

A distant bird call. The air suddenly freezing,
Some soldiers were gasping and spitting.

They all expected something terrible …
Heard, across valley, one shot arrow.

It was seen coming from the crag and down
Hitting the centre of that pie on the ground.

Quarter mile shot, straight as a whisker!
The Captain forgot his brave soldiers' hunger –

Rushed to his horse and he was fleeing,
Straight away the others following.

Leaving the Hawk and men in the forest
And wild rocks forever belonging to the Welsh.

The Act of Union

In 1536, the authorities in London decided to unite England and Wales. This act wasn't a bridge-building move, not an opportunity for give and take and creating a fair chance for all. Oh, no! The aim was to strengthen England's grip on Wales, to make Wales more like England. In fact, the intention was to eradicate, dissolve and eliminate Wales.

According to the act, the Welsh were to obey the king of England and live according to English law. English officials were created to manage daily life in our country. There was a High Sheriff in every county, and his job was to ensure that the English crown became more and more powerful in Wales. Only people who spoke English were allowed to hold public office in Wales. The Welsh language was effectively banned in its own country.

Song of the High Sheriff

In every county of this country
Things are as they should be:
Dinbych is now called Denbigh
And Ceinewydd become Newquay;
The land has been united
From Dover to Holyhead,
United under one crown –
'Yes, Wales, your day is done!'
*   Wales now has come*
*   Under England's thumb*
*   And I am an important man.*

I was honoured by the King
As an English-speaking gentleman,
My name was once ap Sionyn
But 'Jones' is what I've become;
Amidst Parrys, Powells, Pritchards
I take up my residence,
Mansion where I choose my tune,
Sing in the correct language.
*   Wales now has come*
*   Under England's thumb*
*   And I am an important man.*

All the laws of Good Hywel
Have now been made illegal,
The only way mercy can be found
Is to bow to those of England;
I sit strong in high office,
From my castle view the populace,
It is the 'Realm of England' here
And my own ambition's clear.
    Wales now has come
    Under England's thumb
    And I am an important man.

'The Welsh language,' they say,
'Is very difficult to write,
It sounds like the coughing of a bullock.'
This makes me chuckle away.
'Wales itself is so savage
And everyone's dressed in sacks.'
I humour their opinions,
Nod politely, never turn my back.
    Wales now has come
    Under England's thumb
    And I am an important man.

The Drovers of Wales

There is good grazing in the valleys and lowlands of Wales – our steady rain ensures it. This is the perfect country for rearing animals and it's no surprise that we are renowned for farming sheep, as well as beef and dairy cattle.

For hundreds of years produce from Welsh farms has been in demand in towns and cities abroad. Nowadays, Welsh meat is sent in huge lorries to Spain, Italy, Russia and France. But in the old days – even before railways – cattle and sheep, pigs and geese had to be walked all the way from Wales to south-east England for the London markets.

The drovers' job was to drive the livestock to England and get the best price for them at the markets, and then bring the money back home to the Welsh farmers. Drovers had to have a special license, and the work carried a great deal of responsibility. Usually between four and eight drovers travelled together, along with a number of dogs and young servants, driving a herd of about 400 cattle along rough mountain tracks from the west of Wales to the plains of England.

Before starting, cattle would be shod by the local blacksmith and would travel between 15 and 20 miles a day, the journey taking about three weeks. By 1750, around 30,000 cattle from Wales were being driven like this every year.

One of the old drovers' routes starts in the Dyffryn Ardudwy area on the coast of Meirionnydd. It rises over the Rhinogydd mountains, passing a smithy (for shoeing) and an inn called Llety Lloegr (*'the England Inn'*) and then climbs Bwlch y Rhiwgyr (*'drovers' pass'*) before dropping down to the Mawddach valley and Dolgellau.

The Gap of Rhiwgyr

In the England Inn we were last night,
Cattle lowing and clink of blacksmith near
While Ifan the Drover caught the landlord's ea

Milestone on our way over the mountain,
Last stone before crossing Rhinogydd
And with the morning's weather threatening.

Running those horns to the Gap of Rhiwgyr,
Wind from Ireland withering every creature;
Buzzards crying from their airy kingdom.

Up the valley, low clouds gathering,
On the horizon the fingering pines,
Crooked walls and silent ruins.

Leaves carried by the river Sgethin,
Hares speed into thickets of gorse,
Sunshine on the ring of Arthur the King.

Gaze back before departing,
At a trail of black and tops of mountain
Leading to Llandanwg beach, to home.

The Gwydir Family

One of the aristocratic Welsh families who gained favour and great wealth during the Tudor Age were the Wynns of Gwydir, in the Conwy valley. They were rewarded with lands for supporting the king, taking over Maenan Abbey. But they also enlarged their estate by illegal and deceitful means.

A local story tells of one of the Wynns putting earth from Gwydir's garden in his shoes, in front of his lawyer. They both go and stand in a field in front of a local farmer, the nobleman proclaiming: 'I stand on Gwydir soil.' His lawyer confirms this, and the farmer surrenders the field to the estate.

But there is another local story about an old woman getting revenge on one of the Wynns by cursing him, after some similar deception. According to the story in this ballad, the day a deer was seen on the lawn of the mansion was the day this Wynn died.

Old Woman and Wynn o Wydir

'Revenge will come, Wynn o Wydir,
For stealing that white mansion:
Deer will invade your lawn
And weeds stake their claim.

You can raise the height of your walls,
You can mark the boundaries around,
But Conwy's fiercest winds
Will bring your trees to ground.

At the breaking of the dawn,
When the druid-oak is alive,
There'll appear a gap in your fence
Through which those deer will arrive.

As you sleep, a large wild stag
With death between its horns;
Peace will return to the valley
When all your treachery's gone.'

The words made the widow tremble
Despite her mind of stone;
Yes, walls grew – yet after the storm
Deer came to graze on her garden ...

Translating the Bible into Welsh

Welsh is one of Europe's oldest literary languages – poetry was being sung and written in the language long before a single word of English, French or German, or many other European languages, existed.

Perhaps the most important literary achievement in the history of the Welsh language was the publication of the first Welsh Bible. By 1567 William Salesbury had already translated the New Testament into Welsh. Bishop William Morgan, when still the parish priest of Llanrhaeadr-ym-Mochnant, built on the work of his predecessor. However, he set about translating the whole Bible into fluent and refined Welsh, and steered it through to publication in 1588.

William Morgan was brought up in Tŷ Mawr Wybrnant, near Penmachno, and was educated

locally before being sponsored by the Wynn family of Gwydir to go to Cambridge University. Not only expert in Greek, Hebrew and Latin, he was also a master of literary, poetic Welsh. It took him six years to translate the Bible into the Welsh prose that became the basis for modern Welsh.

In William Morgan's day, the Bible had only recently been translated into English and was being read in every church in Wales on Sundays. He and others argued that people were getting no benefit from this, as they knew no English. There was a need to translate the Bible into Welsh, he said.

There were no printing presses in Wales at that time, so the work had to be done in London. It was decided to place a Welsh Bible in every parish church in Wales, but the London printers did not understand a word of it!

William Morgan went to London in the company of a group of drovers from Wales. He spent a whole year organising and editing the printing work. As with the drovers, his aim was to bring the treasure home to Wales.

The new Bible was easy to read and its arrival was exciting for audiences in Wales. William Morgan used dignified and powerful language and it became the foundation for Welsh authors for centuries. Generations learned to read using his Bible, and that gave Welsh publishers a tremendous boost.

In the Beginning

A man, a candle and words in the dark
Searching for Matthew, Moses and Mary's path.

Paper, quill and wax in the loneliness,
All shaking the orchards of Welsh.

Ears, eyes and hands in the silence
Listening to language's long night voice.

In the beginning such a tenacious fight
Against exhaustion, the words bringing light.

Griffith Jones' Circulating Schools

Between 1546 and 1660, there were 108 books published in Welsh, but between 1700 and 1799 there were 2,500. That's a huge increase – 25 books a year instead of almost one! There was at least one printing press in each market town in the country by the end of the eighteenth century and the works produced were mainly in Welsh. In the same way as the World Wide Web and new social media allow us today to gather and share information, so the printing presses of the eighteenth century produced material that was read and discussed and which opened up new avenues.

These publications would have been useless had not the people been able to read the books, magazines and verses being published. Something remarkable happened in Wales in this period – over 300,000 Welsh people, young and old, learned to read. That's three quarters of the population of the country. By the end of the century Wales was the most literate country in Europe, and its educational system was widely recognised, with countries like Russia trying to replicate our success in creating a reading mass population.

One man was essentially responsible for this feat: Griffith Jones, Llanddowror (1683–1761). He was raised in rural west Carmarthenshire and, after a period in the village school, he herded sheep. There was no free education from the state at that time – only children whose families could afford to pay received an education. Griffith Jones' family managed to send him to Carmarthen (*Caerfyrddin*) grammar school in his teens, and at twenty-five he was ordained to the priesthood. He was a very inspiring preacher, a master at expressing himself in the Welsh language. He preached in churchyards, as huge crowds would spend hours listening to him, far more than would fit into the churches.

In middle age, Griffith Jones came to the conclusion that preaching alone was not enough to teach the everyday folk. He realised the need for ordinary people to learn to read the Bible and other books for themselves. The ability to read shouldn't remain as a privilege just for priests. Griffith Jones hit on the simple but effective plan of circulating schools and at 48, despite being in poor health, he devoted himself to this, his life's work. His plan was this: to have the priest or a person in authority invite a visiting teacher to hold a school in a suitable building within a specific locality in the country for three or six months between September and April, when the agricultural year was quietest. Teachers were trained at Llanddowror by Griffith Jones himself and received a small salary from a charitable fund. After spending a term in one location, the teacher would move on to another, with the brightest pupils from the original school keeping it running and often becoming teachers in neighbouring districts as well. Both children and adults came to the classes. The number of schools grew so quickly that there were over two hundred running a year. By the time Griffith Jones died, more than 3,500 circulating schools had been supported. The Sunday schools continued this work.

As well as becoming the language of reading folk, Welsh also helped to return a Welsh character to areas such as the Vale of Glamorgan, one of the areas which, since Norman times, had lost the language.

The Blacksmith's Words

A blacksmith from the village was in class today,
Pulling up a chair, sitting down heavily,
Picking up the Bible as though a feather,
Clutching it with his black hands firmly.

Staring at the print and tracing the rules,
Rusty as the tips of his old tools,
Hearing those vowel sounds in the room
Like blowing bellows, not language spoken.

Soon there were sparks in his eyes,
Hands slackened as he became wise
To the letters' purpose, just as he'd made
The iron carvings on the church gate.

He saw, as in the forge's fire,
Parts assembled from scrap everywhere;
When the lesson turned, so consonants rang
Like horseshoes wrought with hammering.

A Pirate from Wales

Robert Edwards from Wales and his crew of uncouth pirates made a great deal of trouble for Spanish trading ships at the start of the eighteenth century by attacking them and stealing their treasures. This came to the attention of Queen Anne, who was on the throne at the time. But Robert the pirate wasn't punished, he was rewarded. England and Spain were enemies and, on the quiet, the English crown was very grateful that so many pirates were threatening Spanish shipping.

Robert Edwards' reward was a piece of land on an island in the Hudson estuary on the east coast of America. Back then the gift was 77 acres of mud and clay and sand. Today, lower Broadway, Wall Street and Hudson and Greenwich stations in New York stand on the pirate's land – these few acres are part of Manhattan and are worth 800 billion dollars.

Robert Edwards had no interest in building a city. The land was leased for 99 years to John and George Cruger on the understanding that it would be returned to the Edwards family at the end of that period. Robert departed for Europe in 1778, but his ship was wrecked in a storm. All lives and all property were lost in the wreck, including the pirate's lease documents. In 1877 the lease expired on the New York land and a controversy started about who was the real owner of the site.

Trinity Church, New York occupied the land by then and, to date, that body has managed to successfully fight off the Edwards family's claim to the land. Three thousand of Edwards' descendants in America and two thousand in Wales have sought to prove that they are related to the old pirate and that this strip of land in Manhattan is their estate.

On the other hand, a native American tribe have an interest in 'Manhattan' too. In their language, the meaning of *manah* is 'island' and *atin* is 'hills', so Manhattan is 'Hilly Island'. According to an old story, their forefathers sold Hilly Island to early Dutch traders for a few beads. And some of that tribe also want a fair price for the land today.

The Pirate's Island

If Edwards is your family name
And you are of Welsh origin
And you'd like to make a fortune
From a piece of Manhattan,
Then come and join the game!

Robert was a pirate and fierce one
Who set upon the ships of Spain;
Who, according to the legend,
Received an award from the queen –
That's how it worked out then.

His gift, 77 acres complete
On the island between sea and sea
Where today's the site
Of Broadway and Wall Street:
The golden Big Apple indeed.

Worth £800 billion now in dollars;
Back in 1762, however,
There was only a muddy river,
Overgrown banks of the Hudson
Hardly an island of treasure.

Robert was heading back home,
A lease of 99 years
Made out to John and George Cruger
So that, eventually,
His family would gain the money.

The pirate's last journey was shipwrecked,
Under sea his whole world drowned,
He died there
With that document underwater –
His rights to the land gone.

He had 6 brothers and 1 sister:
In 1877 their ancestors
Sought out solicitors,
But Trinity Church was plotting
With its own ideas.

There are 5,000 in Wales
Who have claims on that part of the USA
And courts have shown
Their rights to the island,
That they are owed a fortune.

Perhaps if you're an 'Edwards'
From Pembroke, the Valleys or Gower,
Like those pirates of old
In the stories told –
You own Manhattan – who knows?

'No!' says a salty voice in the distance,
 'Manna is my people's country,
Hata the hills beyond deed –
That place and its worth,
Ancient, sacred, our truth.'

A New Wales

The years 1650–1800 were a period when many from European countries went to the 'New World' in north America in search of a freer life. In Europe, religious, cultural and social divisions were bearing down on many sections of society and there was a new longing for freedom.

But sailing to America was seen as fleeing by others – they preferred to see if it was possible to improve the situation in their own countries.

The *Eisteddfod* was revived in this period. In Maelgwn Gwynedd's time there was a long history of poetical and musical competition, and the Lord Rhys held the first Eisteddfod in 1176. The eisteddfod tradition was revived in the eighteenth century. By the 1730s they were fairly common events, mostly held by bards in taverns. In 1792 Iolo Morganwg – seeking to restore contact with the old Celtic druidic culture – held a Gorsedd of the Bards on Primrose Hill, London. From 1819, the Gorsedd and the Eisteddfod joined forces and so began a national cultural festival that became Wales' parliament and university for a considerable period.

Iolo Morganwg

Three things I love greatly:
The language and its expressions,
Sun's face which shines brightly
*And the company of ancient 'englynion'. **

Three things are in my intentions:
To make my name renowned,
Call out 'Peace!' with rousing sound
At a festival to transform everything.

Three things are hateful to me:
King like an angry ghost accusing,
Those who lie and also lead,
Any insult to the name of 'Morgan'.

Three things should never be still:
The restless wings of imagination,
Stones' shadows on top of a hill
And white bird of poet's musing.

Three things are clear to me:
We must escape the cage,
Fly out of the gloom of history
Into the light of a new age.

* Traditional Welsh verses.

Industry in Merthyr Tydfil

Change was so rapid after 1780 that historians refer to what happened as a 'revolution'. The new age turned its back on the old agricultural way of life in the countryside and put prestige on heavy industries such as iron, coal and engineering. This was the Industrial Revolution and south-east Wales was one of the early centres of that revolution. By 1851 over half the population of Wales depended on heavy industry such as copper, coal, slate or iron and steel rather than agriculture. Amlwch controlled the price of copper on world markets and later Cardiff set the global price for coal. That meant that Wales was the first industrialised country in the world. Although many emigrated from Wales to the 'New World', on the whole, the country retained its young and enterprising people within its own borders, creating Welsh-speaking industrial areas were Welsh culture thrived.

But there was a price to pay. Several ironworks were opened in Merthyr Tydfil, including Dowlais. The town changed completely. It was a bustling, industrial town by 1800, with 7,705 people living there. By 1840, the population had grown to 35,000 and it was the largest town in Wales. There were over three thousand Irish in Merthyr by 1851, and 'Chinatown' was the name of one of the dirtiest and poorest areas.

The ironworks were owned by families from England, and the Crawshay family of Yorkshire was the most powerful. In 1825 William Crawshay spent what was a fortune at the time building Cyfarthfa Castle for himself and his family: a luxurious home of 72 rooms.

Although good wages were to be had in the ironworks and families had been drawn there to avoid poverty and hunger in rural Wales, Ireland and parts of England, life was very hard in Merthyr. Terraces of small houses were built too close together without clean water and in the shadow of the iron furnaces. Yellow smoke from the works descended over the town in toxic clouds and rubbish and sewage were thrown out into the street. No one cleaned the street or collected the rubbish. Everywhere stank terribly and infection and disease spread quickly through the town.

The great misfortune for these families was that life was healthier and better in the rural areas on which they had turned their backs. By the time they had paid for their work tools – even having to pay for candles by which to mine coal from the pits – and paying high prices for goods in the companies' shops, many of the workers were in debt and having to work harder still under punishing conditions.

Chinatown, Merthyr

Under back doors snow is creeping,
In the cold babies are wailing,
There's yet another funeral procession
In the bitter wind from Dowlais.

There are two men fighting in the street,
Cursing each other as they bleed,
Children waiting, always in need
In the bitter wind from Dowlais.

Toiling long hours to buy the food,
Caught in a net it's hard to move,
Grey with old age far too soon
In the bitter wind from Dowlais.

Hooked by the ironmasters' lines,
Bought and sold in their prime,
Longing for countryside left behind,
In the bitter wind from Dowlais.

A Press Gang on Bardsey

Much of Merthyr's iron was used to build and equip the British Navy for its wars worldwide. There was a long period of war against France in the early nineteenth century – and that meant a lot of work for the furnaces of Merthyr.

But in order to fight their wars, empires down the centuries had forced men to join their armed forces. The rabble that had – for about four hundred years – compelled coastal men to join the British Navy was the press gang. For hundreds of years that was the only way they could secure enough sailors to endure the difficult and dangerous condition of their warships on the world's oceans. The practice ended after Napoleon's defeat in 1815.

The sailors' wages were very low: about half that on merchant ships and of agricultural workers. The food and the living conditions were appalling and, of course, there was a high risk of being killed. To have enough men, the navy had rough gangs to round up vagrants and the occasional drunk in pubs and drag them to the warships in the harbour. Having been 'press-ganged' like this, they would be owned by the navy for as long as required.

During the Napoleonic wars, one of Britain's massive warships – a 'man-o'-war' – dropped anchor near Bardsey (*Enlli*). The island's men – men of the sea and boatmen every one – had never seen a warship that close before. They went out towards her in their rowing boats and as they drew near, they were invited to board and have a proper look round. In all innocence, they accepted the invitation.

Suspecting nothing, the Bardsey men climbed the ropes to the deck. Only one of the islanders could speak English at that time – a character called Siôn Robert Gruffudd. Speaking with the ship's officers, Siôn Gruffudd realised that he could make a pretty penny by betraying his neighbours. The rate for press-ganging was shillings a head: the 'king's shilling' was the saying. Evidently Siôn sold the island men to the warship on condition that he be allowed to escape.

Siôn Gruffudd returned to the island but it wasn't long before the women on the island realised he was a traitor. He fled and looked for a place to hide as the women combed through every hole and cave on the island with the intention of catching and hanging him for the betraying their menfolk to the man-o'-war. Siôn managed to escape from the island somehow. Some say he fled to America. He was never heard of again.

News of the kidnapping reached the mainland and someone in authority – possibly the lord at Glynllifon – raised the matter with the Ministry of War. When it was stressed that a whole community of islanders would starve unless the Bardsey men were returned, the navy acquiesced. To the delight of the mothers and daughters, the men came back to the island.

Rage of Bardsey's Women

Silver coins of the gloomy King
Fill the purse of Siôn Gruffudd;
A man-o-war in the bay
All for royal money
And those who serve loyally
Just like Siôn Gruffudd;
It will not be there any more
If we capture the neck of Siôn Gruffudd.

Our Bardsey boys are locked up
And the ship is rolling;
The man-o'-war ready to leave
And Bardsey boys are slaves,
But there'll be a war
Full of smoke and fire
When we capture that hawk Siôn Gruffudd
And break every bone in his body.

Night will come like a dark cave,
Like a boatman's cage,
Every home knowing
We must catch the traitor
Before he runs;
Raise the gallows on the mountain
With a rope ready for Siôn.

The small boats are empty here
Just as all the fields are,
The man-o'-war with royal ensign
But our boats are full of nothing
With their nets torn
And oars too heavy;
We'll send a curse across the land
For winds to wreck that Siôn.

Riot

A period of great changes often leads to injustice and dissatisfaction. This happened in the wake of the Revolution in Wales' industrial areas: trouble over people's rights led to mass protest and sometimes violence. The most famous was the Merthyr Rising in 1831, when troops fired into a crowd of workers. The crowd turned on the soldiers and this led to the hanging of Dic Penderyn. There was another uprising in 1839 in Newport (*Casnewydd*) when a large contingent gathered to protest against food shortages and because workers lacked the vote. In front of the Westgate Hotel soldiers again shot into a crowd, killing more than twenty demonstrators. In over a century of industrial unrest, the British Empire sent its troops to quell ordinary workers in Wales several times.

There were riots in the countryside as well. Poverty was at the root again – prices for agricultural produce were low, there were several poor harvests, and the turnpike companies charged exorbitant tolls. Permission had been granted to companies to improve the roads and charge road-users a toll, and so much a head per animal. A gate was placed across the road to stop the traffic so the companies' employees could collect the toll before opening the gate. Next to the gate was the keeper's

cottage. Many of the turnpike companies were English, and kept increasing the tolls even though the state of the roads remained deplorable.

In 1839, a band of farmers and smallholders from west Carmarthenshire and the Preseli area of Pembrokeshire decided to attack the Efail-wen toll gate and house. They meant business, destroying the gate and the gatekeeper's cottage with axes and other implements and burning them. To hide their identities, the farmers put soot on their faces and wore women's clothes. This was the first attack by 'Merched Beca' ('*Rebecca's daughters*').

Over the following years, the riots spread through west and central Wales. Despite the deployment of a contingent of constables – and even soldiers – to these areas, the countryside was behind Merched Beca and eventually the insurgents forced the government to address some of their grievances. In some areas, Beca and her Daughters acted out a little drama when they came to the gate they wanted to demolish. There were over 500 attacks by Merched Beca on gates and other targets.

Daughters of Rebecca

Beca: *The road's full of pot-holes, daughters,*
It's hard for me to journey here,
Prices are too high in the market
And the working day brings anger.
But what's this white house of turnpike?
I've not encountered this before,
There's a barrier in our way, daughters,
We cannot get any further.

Daughters: *Let us see it, Mam –*
It stops you from carrying on.

Beca: *It's huge and heavy, what is it daughters?*
I am old and can't see clear,
I need to get home soon,
The day has been too long.

Daughters: *Can we move it for you, Mam?*
We know you need it done.

Beca: *Wait now… I'm near, daughters,*
I'm finding my way with care,
I truly think this gate's put up
Just to stop my journey.

Daughters: *A large, heavy gate across the road,*
But we have axes and picks ready.

Beca: *Carefully, carefully, my daughters,*
Let's open and try to go onward.

But no, a strong bolt and lock
And it darkens by the hour.
What will we do, daughters,
With our progress totally blocked?

Daughters: *There's only one choice left, Mam,*
                       We'll have to smash the gate down!

Beca: *Then bring it down, daughters of Beca,*
           It has no right to be here!
           Take hammers and smash it to splinters,
           Take picks and axes to destroy the tollhouse
           So we can go freely on the roads.

Destroying the Chartist Mural

Newport Council decided to demolish a wall near a city-centre car park in 2013. There was a storm of opposition – letters to the papers, blogs expressing disappointment, a Facebook campaign and a public protest on the site one Saturday in October. 'Public safety' was the reason the Council gave. Why did pulling a wall down create such an outcry?

There was a mural on the wall – a 200,000-piece mosaic created in 1978 by the artist Kenneth Budd to show the history of the Chartists' march to Newport in 1839. The artwork told a story – and, obviously, that story was close to the hearts of the city's people. Why was that piece of history so important to them?

The Chartists were a group who raised their voices against injustice. They had drawn up a list of changes they wanted Parliament to effect and had collected tens of thousands of signatures. They presented it as 'The People's Charter'.

Their main grievance was the electoral set-up – at that time there were many industrial areas of Britain, but the democratic system did not reflect this. The thriving, heavily populated valleys had no members of parliament, while de-populated rural areas continued to be well represented. The 'Chartists', as they became known, wanted a secret ballot for all men over 21 years old and the right for poor people to become members of parliament.

Many workers from Glamorganshire and Monmouthshire joined the Chartists – they felt they had no voice. It was arranged that three columns of protestors would march down three valleys on 4 November 1839 and converge in the centre of Newport to listen to speeches.

But soldiers were waiting for them at the Westgate Hotel in the city. There was a skirmish and the soldiers fired on the marchers. Twenty-two Chartists were killed and many more injured. Over the following months, at least 250 Chartists were caught and accused of being traitors. Three leaders were sentenced to death but this was later commuted to transportation to Australia.

But that was not the end of the movement. The people of Monmouthshire remember the history and remember the reasons. In time, five of the six points in 'The People's Charter' became law.

By protesting about the destruction of the Chartist mural the people of Newport were defending their right to know their own history and to honour those who were slain fighting for justice.

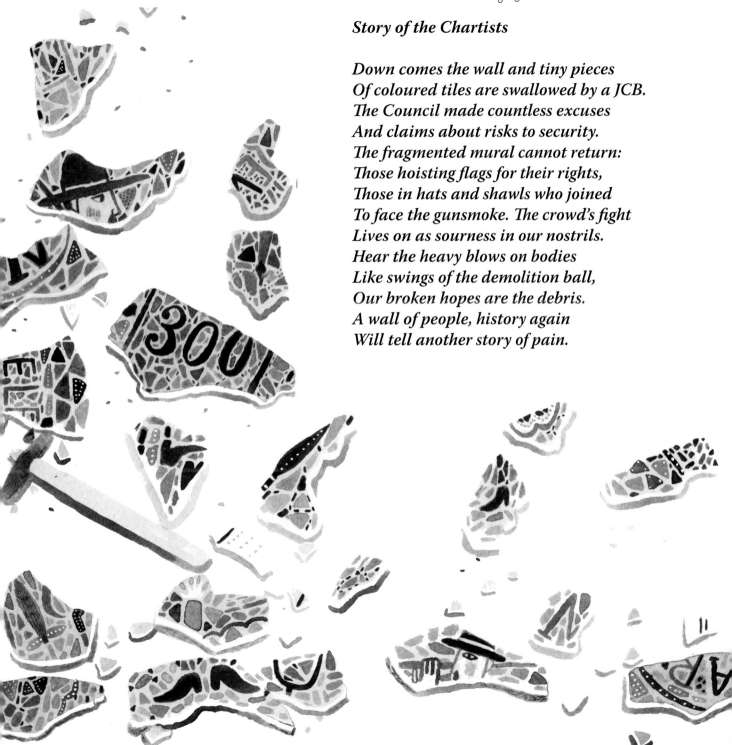

Story of the Chartists

Down comes the wall and tiny pieces
Of coloured tiles are swallowed by a JCB.
The Council made countless excuses
And claims about risks to security.
The fragmented mural cannot return:
Those hoisting flags for their rights,
Those in hats and shawls who joined
To face the gunsmoke. The crowd's fight
Lives on as sourness in our nostrils.
Hear the heavy blows on bodies
Like swings of the demolition ball,
Our broken hopes are the debris.
A wall of people, history again
Will tell another story of pain.

Barbaric Wales!

Because of the Beca disturbances and agitation in the industrial areas, some London people believed the Welsh to be savages! 'Give them some education!' was the view. Welsh was the language of Beca and her daughters; Welsh was the language of Dic Penderyn and his fellow ironworkers and miners. In 1846 an MP rose in the House of Commons and said the children of Wales should learn English to get on in the world.

Three Oxbridge-educated barristers were asked to survey the state of education in Wales and prepare a report. Three Englishmen and three churchgoers: Johnson, Lingen and Symons. They had not a word of Welsh between them, nor any understanding of Welsh chapel life.

These three Englishman travelled through Wales, visiting schools and Sunday schools, and on April Fool's Day 1847 their reports were published, in blue covers. The conclusion was that the children of Wales could not read or speak English – and their teachers weren't much better! The three Englishman emphasised their own views and those of church vicars, but there was very little evidence gathered from chapel ministers. Much blame was placed on the Welsh language – it was undesirable and outdated and a hindrance to

children, said the three Englishman.

Well, you can imagine how many people in Wales were hopping mad at such a report. The Welsh-language newspapers and magazines were full of angry letters from teachers, ministers and bards. Because the reports' covers were blue, the work became known as the 'Treason of the Blue Books'.

One response was that the poets trumpeted more patriotic poems, praising the brilliant literary and musical traditions of the Welsh. Who were these three Englishman to paint us as savages! In 1856, Evan James of Pontypridd composed the famous words 'Mae hen wlad fy nhadau…' ('land of my fathers…'). His son James James composed a tune to the words and this grew to be a popular song. It is sung by crowds at eisteddfodau and rugby matches, and was eventually recognised as our national anthem. 'O bydded i'r heniaith barhau' ('oh may the old language survive') is the rousing finale of the chorus.

But some Welsh people began to heed the accusations of the Blue Books as well. Was it true that the Welsh were falling behind because they speak Welsh? This was the start of the rot in the mindset of Welsh people: they could not see the value in their history, their artistry, or their own tongue. Within a few years, this led to Welsh being banned in schools.

Land of the Blue Books

'Welsh is the tongue of minions
Who carry water from the spring,
Who clear out sties of pigs
And plant potatoes then,'
Say three Englishmen of the Blue Books.

'Welsh is the tongue of maids
Content to scour the pans,
Feed the calves from buckets,
Brush the dirt from carpets,'
Claim those three Englishmen.

'Welsh is full of devilry:
Ancient and lame, dark vocabulary,
Worse still is their poetry
Made dreary by mythology,'
The three Englishmen say.

'Welsh is destroying the pupils,
Keeping them in ignorance,
It prevents them from getting on
In our new civilisation,'
Insist those three Englishmen.

Yet children all over the country
Sing louder than any traitors,
Showing their love of history,
Their voices rising higher:
'Welsh is … and will always be!'

Public Voting

On election day, voters get a piece of paper on which to mark a cross next to the name of the candidate they support. It wasn't always like this.

The practice in former times was that a crowd assembled and those who were entitled to vote raised in their hands to support the candidate's name as it was announced from the platform. At one time, only the truly rich had the right raise their hands to choose a member of parliament. But things began to change and by the 1859 general election many small farmers were entitled to vote.

Back then, very few farmers owned their farms. Rich families owned the land and the rest would pay rent to live and work the farms. In this particular election, many of the farmers voted Liberal, despite the fact that the landowners supported the Tories. This was a very brave thing to do because there was no a secret ballot – just a public show of hands.

The Liberals won many seats and a number of landlords were so enraged that they turned some Liberal-voting farmers out of farms on their estates.

Michael D. Jones, the great patriot originally from Weirglodd Wen, Llanuwchllyn, supported the Liberals' political changes of that period.

The rich landowner Watkin Williams Wynn lost his parliamentary seat, and in revenge turned a number of his tenants out of their

homes. One of those was the widowed mother of Michael D. Jones.

Hands

Long days on fields of toiling,
Ones belonging to Watkin Williams Wynn,
Sowing and reaping
Just to pay the rent,
Putting up gates and fencing
On the widow's smallholding, Weirglodd Wen.

Took a chance after then
To defy Watkin Williams Wynn:
A risk worth taking
To go walking in Meirion
A time to be young again:
Says the widow's son of Weirglodd Wen.

You can put one of those bargains
In the auction of Watkin Williams Wynn:
They cleared the estates
Of the danger of infection,
Scrubbed every single stone,
Taking them from the widow of Weirglodd Wen.

In the hands of these times
Lay the power of Watkin Williams Wynn,
To overturn tables
And empty fields,
Yet a pain never-ending
Was that of the widow of Weirglodd Wen.

Emigrating from Wales

Between one hundred and two hundred years ago, many families and young people chose to leave Wales and venture overseas to seek a better life in the New World. Some went to America, Canada, New Zealand and Australia and others headed for Patagonia in Argentina, in south America, hoping to farm their own land or earn good wages in steelworks and coal mines, or in quarries.

It was not easy to leave Wales and abandon family and friends forever. Sea journeys were perilous and the ships were often overcrowded breeding grounds for infections. But life was hard in Wales too – poverty and hunger; overbearing rich landowners and the established church; small farms and large families.

Tens of thousands emigrated from Wales, largely through the port of Liverpool. They would pass the Welsh coastline and its lighthouses on their journey. They were scattered in new continents and while some were exceptionally successful, others experienced disappointment and loneliness. The grass was not always greener after all, and longing for the old country and the old culture overwhelmed many an emigrant.

Leaving Wales

Dark Mersey river at the boat's stern,
Western sunset on every ridge and mountain,
The sails are full of laughter
And a wind that's rising,
Heading for a golden horizon
With dreams of tomorrow clear.

> *Light of Point Lynas,*
> *Light of South Stack,*
> *Small light of Llanddwyn*
> *And Enlli as we're leaving.*

Easy to see a new path as we nose out to sea,
Hard to look back at the land behind me;
White birds of the shore have gone home
To nests on rocky Pendinas and fields of Blaen-ddôl.

Light of Aberystwyth,
Dim light of New Quay,
Light of Penstrwmbwl
As night comes quickly.

Nobody crossing the bridge on hill's other side,
Forge door shut, getting cold inside;
Mill-wheel stands still at the stream,
Bakery is quiet as it's ever been.

Light of Ynys Dewi,
Lights we can hardly see,
Last lights of Cymru
So dear to me.

Celebrating the Mimosa, 1865

In 2015, in commemorating the 150 years since the first band of 162 Welsh people set sail on the *Mimosa* from Liverpool to Patagonia, many aspects of the story came to life again.

We remember the reasons behind the journey and the venture. In 1865, Wales was a country divided between the common, chapel-going folk and the managers and the wealthy: members of the established church. The chapel-goers gave money to support their own causes but were also obliged – by law – to pay a tithe (a tenth of their income) to the church. Poverty was the great enemy in both rural and industrial areas. Poverty was responsible for illnesses and deaths, for unsuitable housing, and for children ending their education and starting work much too young. Some as young as five worked underground in coal mines.

In 1865 the English and the anglicised Welsh derided the Welsh language and the culture of Welsh people. Welsh was banned from schools, and the mainstays of the culture – such as the *Eisteddfod* – turned to English, as this was thought to be the way to modernise and develop the country. More and more ordinary people got the right to vote, but if they raised their voices or their hands in support of a party not favoured by their landlord, there was

a real risk they would lose their homes and livelihoods.

Indeed, there were plenty of reasons why the idea of a Welsh colony took root in Wales at that time. There had been several attempts to create a Welsh-governed province: in America, South Africa, Australia, New Zealand and even in Palestine. But under the leadership of Michael D. Jones of Llanuwchllyn, the first steps towards realising the dream were taken in the Chubut Valley area of Patagonia, in southern Argentina. Many parts of Wales were represented in the first 162, as well as a number of Welsh people from English towns. On board there were educated people, craftspeople and ordinary workers; rural Welsh and industrialised Welsh. One could call them a truly national assembly.

Freedom propelled them – the freedom to own land, to work without a master, to worship as they wished, to govern their land and society as they saw fit, and freedom to live through Welsh.

It was a difficult enterprise. Their voyage on the *Mimosa* was not a good start: during the two months at sea, they encountered severe storms, disease, and a number of children dying on board. When the party landed at Porth Madryn (*Puerto Madryn*, in Spanish) it was mid-winter: the wind was bitter, and the place was open and bleak, with food and water scarce.

Two-year old Mary Jones of Bala died the day the *Mimosa* arrived in Porth Madryn bay, and became the first of the Welsh to be buried in Patagonian soil. Two weeks later, a daughter was born to a couple from Ganllwyd, and the first Welsh girl born in Patagonia was also named Mary. To remember her, the range of hills around Porth Madryn was named 'Bryniau Meri' (*'the Hills of Mary'*). Little Mary brought hope to the Welsh, hope that they could overcome challenges and make a go of it in that difficult and strange land.

It is so often the case that children bring new hope with them. Today, the Welsh children of Patagonia still breathe new life into the language on the pampas.

The hills of Mary

Wind from the Andes blowing bitter,
Crew without food, heat or shelter,
Pain of having to say goodbye
To a small coffin when they arrived.

But fear and trembling soon left them
When a baby girl was born in Porth Madryn,
They could never forget that morning
With the voice of a newborn calling.

The first born as they left the sea,
Who'd keep alive the words of Cymru,
Who'd repeat the names of belonging
From the old country and different mountains.

Mary the daughter in the coffin,
Mary also the baby crying,
The Hills of Mary, Patagonia –
Sun and tears of our Mimosa.

A Welsh Colony in Patagonia

The party that emigrated from Wales to Patagonia on the *Mimosa* in 1865 dreamed of establishing a country of Welsh character and Welsh in language. It was a huge undertaking, with the early pioneers putting their faith entirely in the dream without knowing much about this land on the other side of the world, or its people. They heard suspicions that the land was unproductive and the native Indians were likely to brutally attack them. But the first group was willing to risk everything – 162 of them boarded the ship *Mimosa* at Liverpool docks on 24 May, 1865: fifty women, twenty-five children, and the rest men.

The settlers landed at Porth Madryn (*Puerto Madryn*) on 28 July, a day celebrated annually ever since in Patagonia as 'Gŵyl y Glaniad' (*'festival of the landing'*). There were white cliffs along the top of the beach and beyond stretched the stony, dusty pampas. The initial period was spent living in caves in the cliffs, but before long the dusty pampas started to be ploughed and a road was opened towards Dyffryn Camwy (the Chubut valley), forty miles away.

The early months were very hard: food was scarce and there was a severe drought. The crop failed in the desert because of their inexperience. Lack of knowledge about the land, the seasons and growth were major obstacles to the settlers, and they feared Indian attacks as well.

Upon arrival in the Chubut valley, small cottages were built of clay and wood and more corn was sown. In October the river flooded and destroyed the crops. The Welsh lived on hunting rather than farming during the first year, and they almost left the valley to move to Buenos Aires, the capital of Argentina.

On 19 April, 1866, two of the Welsh married – the first wedding in Patagonia – but the feast was interrupted by the cry of 'The Indians have come!' However, there were only two of them, on horseback. They approached the company, sitting silently on their horses. There was some language difficulty but understanding was achieved by using a few words of Spanish. The Indians were offered white bread and bara brith (*'currant bread'*), and after seeing that the Welsh were eating it and that it wasn't poisonous, they tried it and greatly enjoyed it. 'Bara' (*'bread'*) was the first Welsh word the Indians learned and for years afterwards they would visit various Welsh farms and ask politely: *'Poco bara?'*

The Indians slept in one of the cottages of the Welsh that night. They left early the following morning and returned in the evening with two women. The four erected a tent – their *toldo* – on the riverbank where they stayed for months, living side by side with the Welsh and teaching them to hunt Indian-style, which kept the settlers from starving.

One Sunday in July 1866 a congregation of Welsh were holding a service in one of their houses when it was surrounded by dozens of Indians. Some of them came in and others stared through the windows. But once again, friendship won the day and a tribe of seventy Indians came to coexist with the Welsh for months. The Indians were particularly fond of hymn singing by the Welsh and would visit their chapels, sitting at the back to hear the singing.

The good relationship between the Welsh and the Indians was something novel in Argentina, where there had been many attacks by both settlers and natives. The Welsh were known as 'Friends of the Indians' in the Indians' language and today in Porth Madryn there is a statue of an Indian scanning the horizon to remember the *Mimosa* and 'Gŵyl y Glaniad'.

Through the Indian's eyes

'I saw this from the top of the rocks
With eyes facing the sun:
Three trees with large white leaves
Across the sea, approaching.

Saw a short-legged creature
Landing upon the shore
Carrying men, women and children
Each looking pale and wan.

Saw these strangers out searching
For water upon the pampas,
The sounds they were making
Were nothing like our own.

They shot invisible arrows
Which made a loud clattering
And away in the distance
A hare fell to ground.

We invited them to our dwellings
Where we shared bread around,
When the cold breath came
We gave them animal skins.

We gathered as friends of the valley
And singing, our hearts rose clear,
Shared with them ancient stories
And our houses and our fires.'

The Mansion Wall

Ty'n Nant is the house and garden at the foot of Nant y Garth, near Felinheli. The remarkable thing about this house is that the wall surrounding the Faenol Estate – a huge wall, seven miles long – takes four sharp bends round its small garden. The house appears to be tucked into the wall. The story behind this is that the owner of the mansion tried to buy the house to build a complete, strong and imposing wall to keep ordinary folk off his lands. Despite every threat and persuasion, the little woman who lived in the house refused to make way for the great man's wall. And to this day the house as like a dent in the Faenol wall.

The Lord and the old woman

'Give me patience and grace… my goodness!'
Said the Lord to his spaniel, in his distress.
'I've lost plump pheasants, rabbits as well,
The poor have poached them, I can tell.'

'They claim a right to cross the river
Through woods and into my land forever.
No peace in our mansion, worries every minute,
We cannot sip tea, not a moment's quiet.'

He addressed his dog, striding his grounds,
'I'll build a long, high wall around;
With sharp stones along its rim,
So the little folk cannot get in.'

Stonemasons came to build it strong,
Lord of the Manor protecting his reputation:
'Spiffingly excellent idea!' noblemen agreed.
'They've stolen our woods!' the people's plea.

Near the main gate to the mansion
Stood Ty'n Nant, an old woman's dwelling;
Red roses around her door, many trees,
Her family had lived there centuries.

If the Lord were to build without a gap,
If he wanted power over all the estate
He'd have to knock down Ty'n Nant
And turn the old woman out.

With guile he tried to buy her home,
When it failed, became more threatening.
Tore down her roses, sent dogs snarling,
But she remained, bravely defying.

Today in that vale, the same wall turns
To avoid Ty'n Nant and its garden.
The dog and its master long gone,
Yet that woman's defiance lives on.

Penrhyn Castle

Penrhyn Castle near Bangor is a fake castle, only about two hundred years old. The family of Lord Penrhyn – who had made their fortune selling slaves and using them to grow sugar in the West Indies – built the monstrous building in 1837. By 1859, Penrhyn was the third largest estate in Wales with a huge annual income of £4.5 million in today's money.

When anti-slavery laws were passed, Lord Penrhyn turned his attention to the slate of the Bethesda area and opened what grew to become the world's largest slate quarry, employing over 3,000 men. Unfortunately, the owners were no more known for fair treatment of the quarrymen than they had been of the slaves formerly abducted from Africa.

The Penrhyn family amassed incredible wealth, spending part of it on the extreme luxury of the castle. Queen Victoria visited the castle in 1859 and for that visit a large four-poster bed was carved from Penrhyn Quarry slate. According to legend, the queen chose not to use that room because the bed too closely resembled a tomb!

The bed can be still be seen in the bedroom, where the south-facing window looks towards the mountains of Arfon and the galleries of the Penrhyn Quarry on the flank of Carnedd y Filiast.

The little Maid of Penrhyn Castle

'Get up out of bed,
This place needs dusting!
You're sleeping like a dead one!

Cap and apron:
The bucket's beckoning!
Marble fireplace needs dusting.

Hot water and cloth
To scrub floors down!
On your knees you belong.

Go now and empty
That brimming potty,
The Lord's drunk enough for his family.

Open the blinds quickly
So visitors can see the quarry!
There's gold dust in its rubble.

Apply your elbow grease
To that slate bedstead,
Bring out a shine in the kitchen.

Think of the slate-workers' style,
Their craft and toil,
Graft and skill of splitting stone.

Soon she'll come here
That Queen Victoria,
Overseeing, relishing the panorama.

Viewing from castle's height
The many galleries
Where quarrymen slog and sweat.

Come now – stir yourself!
Lay the sticks and coal,
No time to waste, it's cold!'

Transporting Heavy Goods

For a while, Merthyr Tydfil was the iron capital of the world – the Cyfarthfa ironworks located there being the world's largest in 1800. There were three other large ironworks in the Merthyr area and the Glamorganshire Canal – almost 25 miles long – was built to transport the heavy bar iron to the port of Cardiff.

Iron was originally used to build and reinforce ships – and for the canons on warships, of course. By the nineteenth century there was great demand for iron for railways, as well as for the steam engines. But before that, some engineer had to invent the 'train' itself – a steam engine pulling vehicles along rails.

Tramways, or 'small railroads', already existed in quarries, smelting works and other works – with wagons pulled along them by ponies or donkeys, or even women and children. But what a great day it must have been when the first steam engine was seen, with its funnel belching smoke and its huge flywheel juddering and turning slowly, drawing tons of weight down the line. This sight was seen for the first time anywhere in the world in 1804, here in Wales. Richard Trevithick was the engineer, and the Penydarren ironworks, managed by Samuel Homfray, the location.

In 1841 the first major railway in Wales was opened, and there is a Merthyr connection here too: it was the Taff Vale Railway. Rails were laid from Cardiff to Abercynon and then onwards to Merthyr, and its opening on 12 April 1841 was celebrated with a public holiday.

First train ever

Dowlais and Cyfarthfa works
Belching out the smoke,
Also Plymouth and Penydarren:
Furnaces, gases, flames;
Bending under the weight
And sweat of their toiling,
To purify the iron
To reach a destination.

Water from foot of the Beacons,
From close by came limestone,
Iron from the mountains,
Coal from the ground beneath them;
At the valley's end a harbour
With a large fleet there
To transport the wealth of Merthyr
To countries everywhere.

The horses were far too slow
To take such heavy loads;
The wagons far too small
Down the hollows and the hills;
Rivers flowed unreliably
To travel with ease and freely;
A canal made, at great cost
Between Merthyr and the coast.

Homfray of Penydarren
Grew tired of this situation;
Crawshay of Cyfarthfa
Another frustrated ironmaster;
They could transport to Abercynon
Along a small road, but the iron
Took far too much labour
And far too much strain.

They'd heard tales of Trevithick
And his steam engine,
Sent word to his native Cornwall
To see if he'd come quick
And try to design a machine
To take the weighty iron
In a long row of trucks
Nine miles from Penydarren.

The challenge to move them quicker
Than they could go on water –
But the boiler would surely explode
That knew that was a fact;
So it was strange to see
That iron horse powered by steam:
Small body and high chimney,
With odd-shaped, rounded feet.

On one February morning
With hundreds ready and waiting:
Ten tons upon the wagons
And large cogs turning
With a deafening sound,
Black smoke – the time had come:
Wheels began crunching –
The world's first ever train!

For four hours and five minutes
There were great groans and fire
As it cut through woods ahead
At the speed of five miles per hour,
It reached the destination
Thanks to a man of innovation,
In the year of 1804
So vital to our future.

One hundred years later
Trains travel this way
At sixty miles per hour:
How small distances became!
There, on the rails of Wales,
With steam, coal and fire
Trevithick's first train
Should've been called 'Inspire'.

Sailing the Llŷn Coast

Because Wales has 750 miles of coastline, the sea has been a key agent in the country's history. The first people to settle here came by sea and Celtic saints kept in contact with those in our neighbouring countries by sea. Enemies came by sea to attack and castles were built with shipping routes to supply them.

Later, ocean-going ships were important in Wales' industrial development: coal and slate, copper and granite were exported to Europe, with some ships travelling as far as America and Australia. Clearly the advent of the train to transport goods and, later, improvements in the roads, mean we are less dependent on the sea and its traffic.

Llŷn, in north-west Wales, was one of the last areas where sailing ships plied their trade between small ports, carrying coal, wood, lime and fertiliser to farms, and eggs, butter, cheese, pigs and bullocks to market. With the mountains of Snowdonia (*Eryri*) an obvious barrier when travelling overland, Llŷn is remote. Almost every small creek and inlet is a port and there are interesting remains to be seen all along the coast. But perhaps the best reminders of the age of sail are the names of these coves. Ships were landed on the sandy beaches, without a quay or harbour, and the

Llŷn name for these beaches is 'porth' (*'port'*). So this is the 'porth' – the portal – between land and sea. There is romance in their history and certainly romance in the old name of each 'porth'.

The shipping shores of Llŷn

When singing a song of Porth Dinllaen
You dream about Flat Huw Puw
Raising spirits on the coast of Llŷn
Bringing the old ways into view;
Cargoes were coming and going:
Lime from Great Orme, southern coal,
Wood from Newfoundland arriving
And, for roads, Nant quarry stones.

Porth Ychain, Porth Llanllawen,
Porth Ceiriad, Porth Cae Coch,
Porth Sglodion and Porth Sgadan,
Porth Gwymon, Porth y Gloch,
Porth Meudwy, Porth Siôn Richard,
Porth Felen, Porth Bryn Gŵydd,
Porth Geirch, Porth Golmon, Porth y Nant,
Porth Poli and Porth Brwyn.

Llŷn's ships across the ocean:
The Margaret Puw and Laura Griffith,
Sabrina, Commodore and Ann,
Their loads essential for living;
White sugar and mill stones,
Manure from Dublin, stacks of crops,
Steamers of Liverpool, the Sybil Wynn
And Phoenix, Fanny Beck and Hope.

Porth Sglaig, Porth Ysgyfarnog,
Porth Hadog and Porth Bach,
Porth Ferin and Porth Foriog,
Porth Al'm, Porth Trefgraig Bach,
Porth Fechan and Porth Lydan.
Porth Wisgi and Porth Fawr,
Porth Hocsaid, Porthor, Porth Tŷ Llwyd,
Porth Iwrch and Porth Tŷ Mawr.

Rings of iron in the rock,
A lime kiln and coal yards,
Leading down are cart tracks
Right to the loading sheds;
Schooner and steamer are waiting,
Crew joke as cattle loaded,
No record of toil and sweat
Only pictures on Tŷ Coch's walls.

Porth Cychod and Porth Cesyg,
Porth Solfach, Porth y Wrach,
Porth Llwynog, Porth y Pistyll,
Porth Glas, Porth Mari Bach,
Porth Iago, Porth Hendrefor,
Porth Tywyn and Porth Llong,
Porth Rhos y Glo, Porth Penrhyn Crydd,
Porth Ddofn and Porth Dinllaen.

Children of the Coal Mines

It was not only men and women who worked in heavy industries during the Industrial Revolution. On sailing ships, in the woollen mills, on rubble in the slate quarries and underground in the coal mines, children had to face serious risks and work long hours to help the family make ends meet. Very few miners indeed were able to work beyond fifty and the industry was heavily dependent on children as young as six years old to open and close underground ventilation doors, carry baskets of coal, haul wagons using chains attached to their belts, and clear debris.

Every Welsh family should experience a visit to the Big Pit National Coal Museum at Blaenafon. There you can go on an underground tour and be lowered in a cage down a 90-metre shaft to the bottom of one of the deepest mines in the history of the industry in our country. A former miner will guide you by lamplight and you can see the doors that regulated the flow of clean air, which was essential to the mine. He will explain that children aged five or six would open and close the doors. They would arrive at their workplace at six in the morning and remain there until six in the evening. Usually their father or an older brother would lead them to their position and tell them to eat their packed meal of bread and cheese so the rats would have no reason to attack them when they were on their own. They would be left in total darkness, as candles had to be paid for. They would have to listen out for the sound of a pony pulling a train of wagons through the tunnel, and open the door in time for it to pass, or be beaten by the haulier for wasting his time. Children would get so tired that some fell asleep on the track, in danger of having their leg broken or worse if a pony and wagons full of coal were to run over them. Rockfalls from the tunnel roof, dangerous gas, explosions, underground water, being dragged along by the wagons' chains, and falling down a shaft in the dark were other hazards. Children suffered the highest death rates in the mines.

For most of the year they saw daylight on Sundays only, which had a detrimental effect on the children's growth. Working in confined spaces and often bent double, miners could often be identified by their distorted bones, which would not have developed properly in childhood.

In many parts of Wales the coal is deep within the rocks. Coal was needed to heat buildings and to produce steam in steam engines to power the ships, trains and factory machinery in Victorian times. In the Flintshire coalfield in north Wales there is a colliery at Point of Ayr (Y Parlwr Du: *'the black parlour'*), which started to be worked in 1865. An excellent name for a mine, but also a terrifying one, don't you think? At its peak, it extended far under the sea near Talacre, the northernmost point of mainland Wales, and it was one of the last deep mines; it closed in August 1996. Only a memorial to the miners and a brass band keep the name of this pit alive today.

Child of the Black Parlour

I am lying on the tramway
Close by the wooden doors,
Sleep closing my heavy eyelids
And my mind is getting darker;
I was up before the morning
Spread its shining light,
Went down the shaft
To where it's always night.

My father's in Mold prison
After striking for one shilling a day,
Loyal friends of Mr Mostyn
Insisted he had to pay;
Such a brave mine owner
With soldiers at his bidding,
While my dad's on bread and water
And I must earn a living.

Sometimes the ground is shaking,
The walls are damp and loose;
I'm only five years old
But have to wear men's boots;
I'm one of three brothers
Who have crossed the threshold,
Here I am, in the dark and cold,
Child of the Black Parlour.

Lord Mostyn is too mean
To give us candles here,
We're in unending gloom
Not even a glimpse of a star;

I'm lying in the blackness
Before climbing back to night
And then the 5 a.m. again
Screaming at me to wake.

Loaded wagons comes down the tunnel,
Noise of pony, clank of chains,
Dic the Haulier puffs like a bellows
Uttering few words as he strains;
I must be alert as possible,
Move quickly as a hare
To open the door for the coal,
Child of the Black Parlour.

Siôn, who's the oldest collier,
Helps me every day
By bringing bread and cheese here
And a small flagon of tea,
I eat each morsel rapidly
Before the rats move in,
All I've got to keep healthy
As dust engrains my skin.

Sunday's a day of sunshine
When I wake I take my time,
Try to enjoy the brightness
Before Monday's harsh return;
I think the week that's coming
Will be the same as before:
Full of loneliness and desperation –
Child of the Black Parlour.

The 'Welsh Not'

One of the most barbaric ways of trying to kill Welsh and create a barrier to its use as an everyday language was to punish children when they spoke it in school. The thing sounds unbelievable to us today – but this happened between about 1780 and 1925.

When a child was heard talking Welsh in the classroom or in the yard, a piece of wood attached to a string would be hung round his or her neck. On the wood were carved the letters 'W.N.', or the full wording of 'Welsh Not'. The wood would remain around the neck of that child until they heard someone else talking Welsh. That was the chance for release, by informing on the classmate and passing on the 'Welsh Not'. In this way, the wood passed from neck to neck all day. The teacher would cane the child bearing the 'Welsh Not' at the end of the school day. This happened every day. By this method, Welsh was thrashed out of the children.

The idea behind this practice was to spread the idea that there was no value to the Welsh language – in education, trade, industry or on life's journey. The old belief was that Welsh belonged to the past and thus hindered the development of the modern world. The language was a barrier, not a key to the wealth of history and a treasury of stories, poetry and place names.

The 'Welsh Not' continued to be used in some schools until the 1920s. Even today, the memory persists. A Llanelli woman recently recalled:

'My grandfather was walloped for speaking Welsh at school in Carmarthen. He never spoke a word of Welsh afterwards. That's a terrible thing to happen, isn't it?'

Bob of Llangernyw (later R. E. Jones of Llanrwst) remembers that his oldest brother Owen was hit for speaking Welsh with him in the yard on his first day at school in the 1920s:

'Really, what sense would there have been in expecting a boy to speak with his brother in a foreign language, a language his brother had no understanding of at all?'

The shadow of the 'Welsh Not' hangs over Wales still. There are those who still claim that it is useless to use Welsh. Nobody gets beaten for speaking Welsh now, but then again it is still difficult to use in many places. But it is good to see that the majority of people in Wales have now abandoned the outmoded idea that the language sabotages a prosperous future. The truth is that its use in all aspects of national life makes us all stronger.

Tearful Owen

'What happened to you, tearful Owen?
Your voice is choking,
You can hardly talk at all,
Eyes puffed and body shaking.

Did you fall over Owen?
Is blood from your leg flowing?
Can't see rips on your clothing –
Why are you so alone?

Did you get a beating Owen?
Did the Penlan boys attack you?
Same old bullies after someone small –
Teach them a lesson, once and for all!

Tell us what happened Owen –
Did a bull chase you in a field?
What was this terrible thing
Bringing sadness so hard to heal?

Merely speaking, tearful Owen?
Simply asking your brother 'Ti'n iawn?' *
Condemned for just a few words,
Guilty of using a forbidden tongue.'

'You spoke Welsh, tearful Owen?
That language that they will have dead?
Welsh of the marked wood and the stick?
– Whatever came over your head?'

* 'Ti'n iawn?' Welsh for 'You O.K.?'

The Great Penrhyn Quarry Strike

Overlooking the Menai Strait stands Penrhyn Castle, a building full of splendour that reflects the wealth of the family that once owned it. The Ogwen valley, Nant Ffrancon mountains and Penrhyn Quarry can be seen from the castle windows. It all belonged to this family. Just over a hundred years ago this was the largest slate quarry in the world – nearly three thousand villagers from the Bethesda area worked there. But relations soured between the quarrymen and Lord Penrhyn. As well as his land and his castle, his Lordship also believed that his employees were his property.

In 1900 Lord Penrhyn spoke not a word of Welsh and an Englishman called E. A. Young was his quarry manager. The quarrymen were Welsh-speaking and Welsh was the language of the Undeb Chwarelwyr Gogledd Cymru (*'North Wales Quarrymen's Union'*). Fairness for all was the aim of the union, but the quarry paid higher wages to workers who toadied to the quarry stewards. Lord Penrhyn refused to listen to the grievances of union members – his only interest was making thousands in profit.

When he sacked 26 workers in a dispute over contracts in 1900, the rift between the quarrymen and the Lord widened. Hundreds of quarrymen came to support the men in court

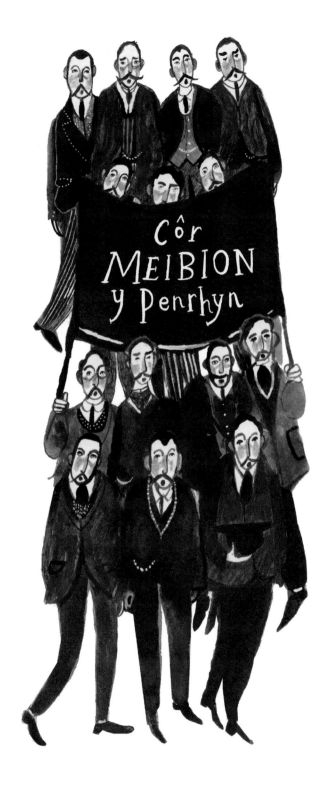

in Bangor on 5 November. Lord Penrhyn was angrier than ever – to teach the quarrymen a lesson for daring to challenge him, he closed the gates and locked the men out of the quarry for a fortnight. The situation was still unfair when the men returned, so 2,800 of them walked out on strike. The strike lasted three years and was known as 'Streic Fawr Bethesda' ('*the great Bethesda strike*'). At the time this was the longest industrial dispute in Britain.

For the quarrymen's families, no work meant no wages. Very soon Bethesda families were short of food. Shops began to close. But Lord Penrhyn was determined to starve the quarrymen so as to force them to submit to his rules.

Many of the strikers left the quarrying area. A number went to work in the south Wales coal mines, sending money home to support their families. There were three choirs in the Bethesda area; they toured to every part of Wales, England and Scotland to hold concerts to raise money for the strikers. As more and more workers in factories, steel plants and mines heard about Lord Penrhyn's attitude, more and more money was collected – over £32,000 in total.

Pennies for the song

We sing with voices in unison,
We sing with strike of stone,
Songs of the chisel and the hammer,
Songs of justice, singing together,
Those who split slate and are strong:
Please give pennies for our song.

We sing about the quarry master
A Lord looking down from afar,
We sing about castles and fortunes,
Sing about the law and its forcing,
Sing about the struggle where we belong:
Please give pennies for our song.

We sing about months without pay,
We sing about mouths going hungry,
We sing about the freezing winter,
Cost of taking children to the doctor,
Sing about homes without clothes and fire:
Please give pennies for our choir.

We sing under the banner of the Union
Or else we'd be weak and alone,
Sing with pride despite being poor
As they trample our rights on the floor,
Sing with hope which is our offering:
Please give pennies for our singing.

The Senghenydd Explosion, 1913

On 14 October, 1913 the air in the Universal Colliery at Senghenydd exploded. Flames shot along the underground levels and up the shaft to the pithead. Rescue teams fought the fire, the smoke, the gas and underground rock falls for weeks; the final death toll was 439 miners and one member of the rescue teams. This remains the worst accident in the history of coal mining in the UK.

Every life that was lost had a story to tell. Sometimes, the figures can make us to lose sight of the individuals and families who are hit by the losses. This ballad is the story of one of those lives lost.

The ballad mentions working a 'double shift'. This means working an extra shift for a partner who is ill, injured or unable to come to the colliery. The worker would do the work in his place and give the wage from that shift to his partner, as there was no other support available to his family at that time.

5 a.m. in Senghenydd

Eic's glad to see the lamps
Though night's the same as day
In the depths of the gallery,
Enjoys fetching bundles
Of lights from the cages.

It's dawn in the village,
Faces of colliers trudging homeward,
Washed ones taking their places
And, among the crowd, Eic sees
His butty Glyn, ready for work.

Glyn and his wife are expecting,
Not sure but it could be soon,
There's a shift to do and he's late;
He must go down to help Eic
His partner and his mate.

As ever the cage is falling,
Scrape of winch, thump of landing,
It's ten past the hour
And Eic is turning for a double shift
Without a word of complaining.

There is a cry from the darkness,
Glyn is racing, a laugh in his voice:
'Our baby sleeps in a cot,
I've held her in my arms, cradled her,
And her mother is doing well!'

With his picture of a new-born child
Lying with cheeks so fresh,
His wife's quiet lullaby;
He carries his lonely light
Into deathly dark of the mine.

Valley Pride

In 2013, to mark the centenary of the Senghenydd disaster, a national memorial was unveiled in memory of all losses in the coal industry in Wales. The list of deaths in various pits and mining areas in Wales is extremely sad: Risca, 1860 (145 lives); Ferndale, 1867 (178); Abercarn, 1878 (268); Maerdy, 1885 (81); Albion, Pontypridd, 1894 (286); Gresford, 1934 (266); Six Bells, 1960 (45); Aberfan, 1966 (116 children and 28 adults).

The composition of the National Memorial statue is of a member of a rescue team helping a miner leave a dangerous pit. Despite many losses, the courage of the rescue teams is still a source of pride. Miners from nearby pits, and those who had been on night shift, made up the rescue teams at Senghenydd. Despite the smoke, gas, explosions, the fire and all the other hazards, they were willing to risk their lives to save their fellow miners. While there was great bitterness towards the mine owners because of their lack of care and safety measures, great admiration persists for the rescue teams' selfless courage.

The Rescue Teams
(Senghenydd 2013)

Commemoration brings the sadness back,
All the tragedy of that disaster,
I pay tribute in white and black
To those who tried to save the colliers,
To those like Jac Ty'n Llyn *
Who returned from fire and smoke;
The gathering and speeches
Brought so much of it back.

The rescue teams down the pit
After travelling over the mountain,
One shaft was full of dust
As they all ventured down it
Into a hell of heat and gas,
The dawn shift at Senghenydd.
The rescue teams braving the mine
After rushing over the mountain.

Imagine the scene they found
Counting hands, fighting through flames;
Twenty-two hours Jac Ty'n Llyn
Saw the corpses lying
In torturing heat below
Which was burning his limbs;
Imagine the dead they found,
Their own comrades and friends.

*Jac Ty'n Llyn and his brother were the last to be rescued from the Senghenydd disaster; they had been trapped underground for 22 hours.

The Villages that Owned the Buses

In the early twentieth century, bus companies began to serve the main towns in Wales, edging out the old stagecoach and horse and cart in areas where there was no train service available. However, some out-of-the-way villages were bypassed by the new transport.

In 1912, two villages in western Arfon joined forces to create a bus company. The villages were Clynnog and Trefor and the bus company was a co-operative: a company owned by local people.

As the buses were red, the company was known locally as 'Moto Coch' ('*red motors*'). But to the people of Clynnog and Trefor, it was 'Moto Ni' ('*our motors*') – as they were the owners. The company remains successful to this day.

'Moto Ni'

From villages at the foot of mountains
To towns, on a long journey,
Only a cart and pony
To take us to destinations;
Dangerous transport, we could see,
Till along came 'Moto Ni'.

We collected enough finance
(Though people were quite poor)
To purchase the first bus
And there were three thousand shares,
The Commer CC553:
Taking to the road, our 'Moto Ni'.

Took it to town for shopping
And back home after,
With so many of us travelling
Businesses thrived more and more;
We easily reached mountain and sea:
Great future for 'Moto Ni'.

Sacks of flour for farmers,
Piglets and calves, amazingly.
Yeast for the bakers
And medicine for the surgery:
Curing our economy
A fully loaded 'Moto Ni'.

Some went on trips to London
Before the motorways came,
Sunday School, Liverpool and even
As far as Calais and Cologne;
Children would shout with glee:
'That red bus is our 'Moto Ni'!'

Driving through all weathers,
Driving for a hundred years,
Familiar as bread and butter
Or a couple of pints of beer;
Carrying hopes and chances to be free:
Our people's own 'Moto Ni'.

The Great War

The First World War, 1914–1918, destroyed far more than the battlefields and the soldiers' bodies. It shattered families, shattered lovers' hopes, and shattered the lives of the many casualties returning home. In the village of Ro-wen in the Conwy valley, eight young men died as a result of the war. And many came back, including four brothers from one smallholding – Fron Haul, on the mountainside – but things were very awkward for them after losing their friends. The four brothers were in the army from 1914 until the end of the fighting in 1918, and one can only imagine the anxiety back home – the 'Edwardses of Fron' home – until the four returned at the end of the war.

Where are my boys?

November, four of the boys
In British army uniforms,
Three began their training,
But the oldest on battlefields of Belgium;
Lads of Ro-wen, in the Blue Bell and Swan
Raise their glasses to Edwards y Fron.

December, freezing cold houses
With winter's heavy burden,
But a letter from Huw to parents
Brings heat to frosty bones;
It tells of a coming vacation,
A welcome smile to Edwards y Fron.

May, a whole missive of verses,
The ink like blood in Huw's veins:
Honour, he says, is to survive
While others around are falling;
Staring into the river with broken
Dreams like twigs, is Edwards y Fron.

October, the battle is fiercer,
Losses piling like dead leaves,
Every week the newspaper column
A memorial to those who've gone;
There's Wil and Joseff and Siôn,
So used to mourning is Edwards y Fron.

June, the Mayor delivers speeches,
The preacher's urging the men;
Fifty more sons join
From Llanbed, Ty'n-groes and Ro-wen:
The band play and boots shone,
But a cloudy head for Edwards y Fron.

April, John returns to Bodawen,
Shrapnel had destroyed his arm;
A breather and break from the guns
Morus Bont Ddu is back home:
Huw has a stick, wants to be alone:
'My heart's like stone!' says Edwards y Fron.

September, the fire at last dies down,
Four are this side of the curtain,
Yet everyone lives in shadows
Of those white, wooden crosses;
'All of our joy and smiles have gone.
Where are my boys?' asks Edwards y Fron.

Peace in the Trenches

The year was 1914. It was Christmas Eve in the trenches in Frelinghien in France, close to the border with Belgium. For the previous four months, there had been a desperate struggle between Europe's greatest armies in those areas, with heavy losses and destruction on all sides. The Germans were settled into deep trenches that stretched from Belgium to Switzerland, and the French and British armies and their allies from around the world were dug into a network of trenches opposite them. In between, there was no man's land with its barbed wire, shell holes and the debris of battle. The weather had been wet and misty for weeks; there was standing water in the trenches and the land had turned into a sea of mud.

But that afternoon, the weather changed. The wind turned colder, and chased the clouds away. Dusk brought wintry stars. The village of Frelinghien was held by a regiment of the German army from Saxony. A little lower down, closer to the river, a regiment from Wales held the line: the Royal Welch Fusiliers.

The moon rose. It was freezing hard and in the trenches the soldiers' feet were like ice in their sodden boots. Over the past few days, parcels of treats had been arriving at the front. The soldiers' families knew that their lads would not be home with them to celebrate Christmas. Gradually, the guns quietened and the assaults declined.

There was an eerie silence under the clear sky. When the last rays of the sun had disappeared, the Welsh Fusiliers were amazed to see paper lanterns and Christmas trees appearing atop the enemies' trenches. Traditionally, in Germany the Christmas celebrations begin on the night before. Across no man's land the Welsh could see heads rising above the safety of the trenches. Normally, snipers on both sides would shoot anyone who stuck his nose above the parapet opposite. The Welsh heard carols and hymns and popular songs sung in the rough voices of the soldiers from Saxony. Not one bullet was fired.

Next day, a thick mist from the river lay over no man's land. The Welsh had lettered Merry Christmas and painted a picture of the Kaiser on canvas and displayed it above their own positions. A few shouts came through the fog from the direction of the enemy. A greeting? Or a threat? The mist lifted gradually and, peering across two hundred yards of battle-scarred land towards the German trenches, some thought that they could see a white flag being waved. A white flag? Peace? Are you sure?

The Germans were the first out of the safety of their trenches, unarmed. They called on the Welsh not to shoot and to come out to meet

them. Some Welsh Fusiliers were uneasy, afraid it was all a trap. But others climbed out of their trenches and quickly crossed no man's land to shake hands with the approaching Germans. Each wished the other well. Gifts were exchanged: beer and cigars from the Germans; corned beef and Christmas puddings from the Welsh. In all likelihood, the Saxony soldiers were delighted with the puddings! Some of the officers joined the ordinary soldiers in shaking hands with German officers and agreeing to a one-day ceasefire.

Similar scenes were witnessed along miles of the Western Front. Dozens of regiments left their positions to greet and chat with their enemies. A football game was played between the Germans and a Scottish regiment in one part of the battlefield. Troops visited enemy trenches and dugouts and enjoy hospitality and friendliness. There was peace and serenity in the trenches.

The war lasted another four, bloody years. The death and destruction was merciless. Millions were killed. But the memory of that remarkable Christmas lived on, a moment when the desire for peace and friendship was stronger than the order to kill.

In 2008 a memorial was unveiled in Frelinghien to mark that day of ceasefire between the Welsh Fusiliers and the regiment from Saxony. The wife of French Prime Minister at the time was present: Madame Pénélope Fillon, who comes from a small rural village near Abergavenny (*Y Fenni*) in south Wales. Frelinghien was chosen as the site of the memorial because that was the only place where officers from both sides met formally to shake hands and agree on an official ceasefire between their regiments.

As darkness fell that Christmas day in 1914, the two armies' soldiers returned to their own trenches. It was clear and starry that night too. Soon, German voices could be heard passionately singing the carol '*Stille Nacht*'. After they finished, Welsh tenor and bass voices were heard singing 'Dawel Nos' ('*Silent Night*'). Two armies, two different languages, but the same carol.

Christmas in France, 1914

On Christmas Eve there were soldiers
In wartime trenches on the French border,
Someone played harmonica and they sang
Voices raised where shells once rang,
Carols about angels, stable and hay,
A baby in the arms of Mary.

On wires they strung lanterns,
In a trench put up a pine,
Mud on uniforms, ice-bitten skin,
Sang of shepherds, manger, wise men,
As the old, old moon shone
Bringing a longing for home.

Two hundred yards away, other carols heard,
Rough choir singing of the same child,
Strange accents, the language alien,
Yet self-same faith as them;
The guns were silenced on that Eve,
An extraordinary outbreak of peace.

Fog between armies at break of dawn,
Shadows emerging, greetings called
Across the waste of no man's land:
'Don't shoot! Come out!' offering hands.
'There's a barrel of beer over here,
Let us celebrate Christmas together.'

Some reluctant to put guns down
For fear the enemy was tricking them,
But seeing courage of those without weapons
Thoughts of ambush were abandoned,
Two armies crossed where many had fallen,
Shared cigars and stories of the season.

All along the front bullets ceased,
Enemies shook hands in disbelief;
Choruses of 'Hosanna,' a football game
And nobody caring who would win:
Soldiers laughed, played, felt free,
That remarkable Christmas of 1914.

Hedd Wyn

Ellis Humphrey Evans – or 'Hedd Wyn' to give him his bardic name – was a shepherd from the Trawsfynydd area, and a poet. He was born in 1887 and grew up on a farm called Yr Ysgwrn. He composed poetry about the people of his district, about nature and the seasons on the Meirionnydd uplands.

1914 saw the Great War, but Hedd Wyn did not have to go to fight because agriculture is essential work in wartime. When his younger brother Bob was old enough, it seemed likely that Bob would be conscripted, as there was not enough work for an extra pair of hands at home. As the oldest son, Hedd Wyn felt it was his place to go. He volunteered and was sent to the trenches. He was killed on 31 July 1917 at the Battle of Pilkem Ridge, at 30 years old.

As a Welsh poet, Hedd Wyn had already made a name for himself by winning four bardic chairs in various eisteddfodau. He was runner-up for the chair in the National Eisteddfod in 1916, and shortly before joining the army had begun composing a long poem on the subject of 'Yr Arwr' ('the hero') for the 1917 competition, to be held at Birkenhead.

Hedd Wyn despised war and composed poems depicting the waste and evil he saw. He spent every spare minute in the trenches completing his poem, and posted it off. In September 1917, when it was announced that Hedd Wyn was the winner, he had already been killed. The chair was cloaked in black and Hedd Wyn has been known as 'Bardd y Gadair Ddu' ('*the poet of the black chair*') ever since.

A number of other lads from Trawsfynydd were killed in the war. And of course, the same sadness was repeated in villages throughout Wales – and throughout Europe. We lost millions of talented youngsters and that lost generation created a huge gap. Here in Wales, Hedd Wyn's story became a symbol of all those lives wasted in the war.

After the Birkenhead Eisteddfod, the 'Gadair Ddu' was carried by train up the Dee Valley and through Capel Celyn to Trawsfynydd. It was placed, alongside his other bardic chairs, in the parlour of his old home. People came to Yr Ysgwrn to offer their condolences to the family and to see the chair. Over the years, Hedd Wyn's mother, then his sister, and then her sons have welcomed visitors from far and wide, showing them the chairs and telling the story. That was their way of giving thanks for the life of Hedd Wyn.

Now Yr Ysgwrn has been presented to the nation, with the Snowdonia National Park Authority as its caretaker. Two rooms are just as they were in Hedd Wyn's day. Visitors are welcome there, as they have always been. The story continues to be told.

Cwm Prysor
Dim ond y lleuad borffor
Ar fin y mynydd llwm,
A swn hen afon Prysor
Yn canu yn y Cwm.
                    Hedd Wyn

Ysgwrn farm

The door of Ysgwrn's open wide
And hearth's flames inviting,
Shepherd's crook above fireside,
Photos on the piano beguiling,
A voice from long ago
Sets the chair rocking.

I hear names of mountain pastures,
Of woods, meadows and streams,
I see from a window here
Moonlight upon the mountains,
Know that whatever the weather
Neighbours enjoyed a welcome.

Others come and sense this place,
A loss like ashes swept away,
Under black beams a silence,
A lamp never lit again;
Before they return to paths
And strangely muted birdsong.

The clock is still tick-tocking,
Oak furniture has a polished shine,
A book on the table's open,
In it there's just one name:
A spirit fills our time
Whispering through this farm.

The Great Depression

As well as the high cost in lives, there was a terrifically high financial cost to the Great War, 1914–18. Britain's war debts have never been cleared – we still pay the price today.

In the 1920s and 1930s, heavy industry – coal, steel, tin, slate, shipbuilding and engineering –saw their worst slump. By 1932, 44% of men in Wales were unemployed. Wages were cut, and there were strikes and closures. After 150 years of industrial growth, there was a 'Depression' – a period of unemployment and mass poverty; food shortages and disease; and young men migrating in search of better opportunities.

This also had a major impact on the Welsh language. Wales lost hundreds of thousands of Welsh speakers. Worst of all, families started to raise their children to speak English, to be fluent when they reached an age where they would have to leave Wales in search of work.

The Glamorganshire and Monmouthshire coalfields were the worst affected in Wales. Between 1921 and 1940, 430,000 people left Wales – 50,000 from the Rhondda valley alone. There was a 40% fall in families' spending on clothing and shoes. In 1928 the government support paid to an unemployed man was £1 and three shillings (£1.15) a week, and two shillings (10p) for each child not working.

After a century or more of ripping its wealth from the ground and the rocks, and Wales was a very poor country.

Because the extreme poverty affected whole families, mothers and wives in Wales were hard pressed. The brave spirit of Welsh women is evident down the centuries and rose once again during the Depression. In February 1934, a contingent of women from south Wales led a Hunger March to London to highlight the poverty and lack of work. This tradition continued through to the miners' strikes and peace campaigns towards the end of the twentieth century – the women of Wales were very much in evidence in these battles too.

Women Marching

They send troops to our Valleys
To put down the miners,
Cause many a row
Between brother and brother …
    So we are marching
    Through town after town,
    Voices raised loud
    With pride of our nation.

They send officials from London
To close our pits down,
See us as columns and figures
Never our needs and faces …
    So we are marching
    Through town after town,
    Voices raised loud
    With pride of our nation.

They send us soup kitchens
To feed our hungry desperation,
Fling us crumbs like starlings
With hardly strength for flying …
    So we are marching
    Through town after town,
    Voices raised loud
    With pride of our nation.

They shut down shops and storehouses,
They're empty as the day is long,
Leaving our children with grey faces
Mouths open like tiny fledglings …
    Yet we are marching
    Through town after town,
    Voices raised loud
    With pride of our nation

The Tirdyrys Fishermen

Saturday 17 June, 1933 was an unusually windy and stormy day, considering that it was midsummer. Three brothers from Tirdyrys farm, Llŷn – John, 26 years old, Elis 21, and Dic 19 – put out to sea in a rowing boat from Porth Gwidlin near Llangwnnadl. Their intention was to lift their crab and lobster pots but, despite them being experienced boatmen, the waves were too much for them that day. All three drowned and their bodies were washed ashore a few hundred yards away at Porth Fesig, below Trefgraig's land. The funeral was held on the following Wednesday in Hebron chapel, and it was the largest funeral ever seen in Llŷn.

Three lads sailing

Three lads sailing from port,
Three brothers in a lively wind,
Steering their boat out to sea
In the thrill of white water,
In surges of the brine
Close to their home of Llŷn.

Three brothers raised on boats
Since they were very young,
Three lads taking the waves
With their usual aplomb,
Three brothers on ocean's plain
Close to their home of Llŷn.

Then tide turns in a crosswind,
Their boat trapped in a trough,
Till the thick fog comes
And everything suddenly changes;
Nobody can hear their calling
Close to their home of Llŷn.

They're flung onto the rocks,
Powerless to do anything,
Victims of tides and the moon,
Three lads with the waves
As graves they are sharing
So close to their home of Llŷn.

John · Elis · Dic 1933

The Fire in Llŷn

On 26 April, 1937 German and Italian aeroplanes dropped hundreds of bombs on the town of Gernika in the Basque Country. The leaders of those countries were helping the fascist Franco during the Spanish Civil War. Gernika is a market town, and an old centre of Basque traditional culture. It had no military defences and, as it was market day on the day of the aerial raid, over 1,500 civilians were killed, including children.

The years of the Second World War saw

'Gernika' repeated across Europe hundreds of times. Bombing densely populated towns and killing millions became an acceptable weapon of war.

Three months before the destruction of Gernika, three men were jailed in London for their part in burning down a bombing school in Wales. The three were Welshmen: Saunders Lewis, D. J. Williams and Lewis Valentine. It was a striking protest against the use of Welsh land to practise for such uncivilized warfare. As soon as the London government announced its intention to establish a training camp for bombers at Penyberth, Penrhos, near Pwllheli in Llŷn, there was a fierce opposition campaign. Letters, petitions, and protest meetings were organised – but the authorities did not listen. Eventually, a small group of nationalists decided that the camp must be torched.

At midnight on Monday 7 September, 1936 the three who were later jailed met four other people at a rural crossroads at Rhydyclafdy, Llŷn. For years, these four accomplices remained anonymous, and then it was revealed that there had been yet another that night too: a local farmer's daughter. She had been a university student at Bangor and was later a Welsh teacher in Llanrwst. Her name was Lydia Hughes, and she had kept an eye on the site and identified paths over the ridge to lead the arsonists to their task.

Song of Lydia Hughes

Cold at the crossroads this evening
Autumn biting into my bones,
On the starry horizon
Bells of the school clock ring;
Wind from Penrhos is unsettling
The leaves and the thorns.

Company at the crossroads this evening,
Deeds which need to be done,
Myths awakened in our minds,
Words of poets make us strong;
A small group, expecting three,
Behind them injustice of centuries.

Resolve at the crossroads this evening,
Everyone waiting so long,
Torches and petrol prepared,
Path over the ridge is seen;
Reaching Penyberth on foot,
The cabins and a pile of wood.

Orange over the crossroads this evening,
The fire's flames are rising,
Heat still in my eyes
Powerful as my nation's remembering;
Their camp of war is burning,
I, a woman, leading not following.

Bombing Swansea

One of the cities that suffered from bombing raids during the Second World War was Swansea (*Abertawe*). It was first bombed in June 1940, and then the three nights of 19–21 February 1941. At that time, Swansea had an oil refinery and a port exporting coal, but the bombs were targeted to cause maximum damage and break the people's spirit. Two hundred and thirty people were killed and over 400 injured. Incendiary bombs were also dropped and flames engulfed the city centre – the flames lit up the night sky and could be seen eighty miles away. Whole streets of buildings were destroyed and 7,000 people lost their homes. The city centre was flattened; walking out of the station you could see clear to the sea in the distance: the once-busy offices and shops reduced to piles of rubble.

Aerial attacks still occur in wars around the world, and people try to seek shelter under tables or under the stairs from remotely controlled bombs.

Note:
The name 'Blitz' for bombing raids comes from the German 'Blitzkrieg', meaning 'lightning war'. In 2008 the American Robert Keim created a new poetic form: the 'blitzverse'. It has no punctuation or rhyme, and moves quickly. It consists of couplets that repeat the first word, and the last word of each couplet loops to be the first word of the next. It is fifty lines long, and starts with a common phrase or a saying and ends by repeating the last words of line 48 and 47 as the final lines. The title is the first word of lines 3 and 47, connected with a preposition. You should be able to read it very quickly, pausing only to breathe.

Hole under the stairs
(Blitzverse)

Call and answer
Call to the hole
Hole in my stomach
Hole of fear
Fear like bee-sound
Fear of noise returning
Returning to whistling
Returning to shivering
Shivering and worrying
Shivering till teeth shatter
Shattering in the street
Shattering next door
Next thing
Next or nothing
Nothing but darkness
Nothing but holding hands
Hands on shoulders
Hands squeezing
Pushing back tears
Pushing away strength
Strength of explosion
Strength in the night
Night in flames
Night which screams
Screams of the siren
Screams from buildings
Buildings falling
Buildings now dust
Dust on my head
Dust of that second
Second becomes an hour
Second of shut-eye
Eyes I must rub
Eyes of the morning
Morning will come
Morning of crying
Crying while searching
Crying through the city
City of nobody home
City of skeletons
Skeleton houses
Skeleton staircases
Stairs to skies now
Stairs going nowhere
Nowhere ...
Now ...

The Beasley Family

At the 2012 National Eisteddfod in the Vale of Glamorgan, one of the stands that attracted the most attention on the Maes ('*field*') was an empty tent. It was to honour Trefor and Eileen Beasley from Llangennech, near Llanelli, and their long battle in the 1950s to receive a rates demand in Welsh, in an area where 90% of the population spoke Welsh. The bare tent evoked the result of their protest: the Beasley family home was emptied several times by bailiffs because of their refusal to pay their debts to the Council until they received service in Welsh.

The Beasley family refused to accept any excuses or give in to threats and after eight years of arguing their case by letter and through the courts, they got their rates demand notice in Welsh. Their stand is now seen as heroic, and as the first case of civil disobedience aimed at securing official rights for Welsh speakers.

Eileen was a teacher from the Whitland (*Hendy-gwyn ar Daf*) area and Trefor was a miner in the Morlais Colliery, Llangennech. They married in 1951 and, in 1952 when they got their first house, they both decided to refuse to pay the rates unless they received a letter from the Council in Welsh. Their case came to court 16 times and bailiffs visited their home four times, taking most of their furniture on more than one occasion. They received a bilingual rates demand in 1960. They had two children, Elidyr and Delyth.

In 1900, half the people of Wales spoke Welsh. By 1951 only 29% of the population did. There was real concern that Welsh – one of Europe's oldest languages – would cease to be a living language. The Beasley's action inspired speeches and a host of protests over Welsh speakers' rights, including the formation of Cymdeithas yr Iaith Gymraeg ('*the Welsh*

language society'). Many laws were broken; many were jailed; many minor victories were gained. But today, the law of the land ensures that Welsh is an official language in Wales.

Furnished with song

Lorry in front of their home.
A black-hatted man
And his strong henchmen
Are knocking, knocking.
Holding an official form.
Piano first to be taken.

Where are they taking it, Delyth fach?
There'll be no more moaning
About doing your practising.

Soon back to grab more,
The mirror from sitting room.
Wedding present, precious as any diamond.
Gap on wall, memory stolen.

What will you do, Trefor,
To spruce up before a meeting
After the dirt of the mine?

This time it's chairs
And their companions, the sofa;
On the street, strewn everywhere.

Where will you sit, Eileen,
At the end of a long day
When you're full of exhaustion?

They're hauling away the carpets!
The floor's left so hard
Every single echo heard.

Where will you find comfort, Elidyr?
Dad reading his paper,
Mam writing her letters,
You on the cold floor.

Yet despite all this
A single family's defiance,
People from Llangennech
Against the lorry, black hat,
Councils, Courts and more.
Though the piano's gone
A quartet of Welsh spoken,
Furnishing a house with song.

Keeping the Waters from Llangyndeyrn

Cwm Gwendraeth Fach is a lovely agricultural vale between Kidwelly and Carmarthen (*Caerfyrddin*). In the summer of 1960, ten thousand cattle grazed a thousand lush acres, and many long-standing families lived on the farms: generations of sons succeeding their fathers. There is poetry in the names of the farms: Allt y Cadno, Fferm y Llandre, Torcoed Isaf, Panteg, Glanyrynys, Ynysfaes.

Then came the news that Swansea (*Abertawe*) Town Council was considering building a dam across the Cwm, to drown the valley and create a reservoir for west Glamorgan's industries. The Cwm people could not believe it! But the threat was real. Wales had already lost a number of valleys to create reservoirs of water for big towns:

Tryweryn, Clywedog, Elan, Claerwen, Efyrnwy (*Vyrnwy*). Would that be the fate of Cwm Gwendraeth Fach as well?

The residents came together in the village in the middle of the Cwm: Llangyndeyrn. Every farmer and all the villagers decided to create a defence committee. The Swansea officials would not be allowed to look at the fields, let alone flood them.

Surveyors from Swansea came in a Land Rover to measure the land. There were locks and chains on every gate in the valley. Behind the gates farm machinery blocked the gateways – tractors, balers and combine harvesters.

The surveyors came back with the police and a court order allowing them legal access to the fields and to dig holes to see where the best place for a dam would be. But the Llangyndeyrn people would not allow them through the gates. Wherever the Swansea convoy – trucks, Land Rovers, cars, cranes and augers – went, there was an army of locals standing behind the gates, holding firm.

It was a long battle. For months the convoy had to be watched out for. When there was someone from Swansea in the valley, the Llangyndeyrn church bells were rung to call the

locals to defend the gateways. Some of their ancestors were part of the Rebecca Riots, standing up against tyranny over a century earlier. Maybe their relations in the distant past had gone into battle with the Princess Gwenllïan in the same valley. Certainly, the spirit of Rebecca and Gwenllïan was very much alive in the area during the battle of Llangyndeyrn.

The people of the Cwm showed such determination that eventually Swansea gave up and abandoned its plan to drown Cwm Gwendraeth Fach. It is a heroic story about a small community challenging a big town, the full force of the government, the law, and the police – and winning! In 1965 there was another big meeting Llangyndeyrn, but this time it was a party to celebrate their victory.

Ballad of Llangyndeyrn

Clerk of the town arrived with forms
Explaining the where and the when,
Saying they were backed by London's laws
To acquire the land without opposition.

Farmers and others disagreed,
It belonged to them whatever the deed,
On Glanyrynys' fertile fields
A sign put up – 'We will not yield!'

Next they came with policemen,
Local lads pulling their caps down,
The gate barred and fastened fast,
They couldn't break in by force.

So many acres in the valley,
Grassland grazed for centuries;
People determined to take a stand,
Let nobody drown their land.

Llandre farm, from father to son,
Torcoed Isaf, knowing the seasons;
Allt y Cadno near church bells tolling,
Panteg and Ynysfaes, with cattle calling.

Children taught to respect the law,
Yet protecting land was so much more;
An old man shouting in mother tongue,
Woman blocking a lorry with her pram.

Battle of Gwendraeth, small yet sublime,
History's echoes travel through time,
Facing a tyrant as had Gwenllïan
And Daughters of Beca in Llangyndeyrn.

Soldiers

A great many youngsters from Wales have joined the armed forces over the centuries – and it is still happening. In many towns in our country, there is little choice for those who want a salary and a career. Many households in Wales continue to suffer losses sustained in foreign wars.

These verses are an adaptation of an old folk song from Scotland, 'Bonnie George Campbell'.

Dai from Wales

In towns and villages,
Many pubs countrywide,
There's a Dai from Wales
Who is saying goodbye.

His photo's on the mantelpiece,
His family's treasure;
Will he bring back medals
Or be taken forever?

His mam is beside him,
Her tears in streams;
His girlfriend is cwtshing,
All her fears concealed.

The street's gone silent,
Stool empty at the bar,
As Dai from Wales
Is sent to another war.

His cap and each button
So shining and tidy,
Such a proper soldier
With gun at the ready.

His photo's on the mantelpiece,
His family's treasure;
No medals for Dai,
He has gone away forever.

Wales' Hope

Ifan ab Owen Edwards realised something important in 1922: that Wales' hope was her children. He set up Urdd Gobaith Cymru ('*Wales' league of youth*') through the children's magazine *Cymru'r Plant*, and before the end of the year the new organisation had 720 members. Its first branch was established in the village of Treuddyn, Flintshire.

His dream was for children to be able to use Welsh beyond home and chapel. From the outset, the new movement was geared towards socialising and fun so that children could play in Welsh. By 1927 the Urdd had over 5,000 members. The following year, two children's summer camps were held for the first time. The Urdd's National Eisteddfod made its first appearance in 1929 and its first National Sports were held in 1932. This is the start of an organisation that grew to make a huge contribution to the lives of children and the vitality of the Welsh language.

There was no Welsh education in those early days, but in 1939 Ifan ab Owen Edwards and his wife founded a private Welsh school, sponsored by the Urdd, in Llanbadarn Road, Aberystwyth. It had only seven pupils when it opened, but by 1945 there were 81 pupils and four teachers. In 1952 the school transferred to the local education authority, and since then there has been a terrific growth in both primary and secondary Welsh-medium schools throughout Wales. There are now 350 children at Ysgol Gymraeg Aberystwyth ('*Aberystwyth's Welsh school*') in a new building at Plascrug. And, of course, tens of thousands of children attend Welsh-medium schools in all parts of Wales.

The Seven

We know the names of the seven
Who sat at desks to learn.

Surely there were soon songs,
Stories of rights and wrongs.

We can guess which poet's lines
Brought pictures to their minds.

Sums heard in their mother tongue
And before the day was finishing

Places on the map of the world
Would be like secrets told,

History of the earth laid out
As though for soles of their feet.

Path of language begun by the seven,
Path of hope that they had taken.

Nant Gwrtheyrn

Today, a new tarmac road leads down the steep side of the valley to the old village of Nant Gwrtheyrn. These days it is the location of a language centre for Welsh learners, comfortable houses to accommodate them, a cafe, heritage centre, and a hall to host all sorts of events. There are interesting paths to the slopes of Yr Eifl mountain or down to the rocky shore to enjoy the area's wildlife and industrial archaeology.

But things were not always so easy in Nant Gwrtheyrn. People have lived there for thousands of years but because it is so remote, life was hard and the path to it was rough, steep and winding – old names for it include the 'Camffordd' (*'bent way'*) or the 'Miga-moga' (*'zig-zags'*).

There are hill forts in the area, and the bones of a very tall man were found in a mound called 'Bedd Gwrtheyrn' (*'Gwrtheyrn's grave'*). According to legend, a king, Gwrtheyrn (*Vortigern*), fled here from the Saxons. Beuno and his monks came here during the Age of the Saints; the valley was home to shepherds and fishermen; and the legend Rhys and Meinir is associated with its history. Quarries were opened and for a while it was a busy industrial area, with many Irish people coming to work; then the quarries closed and the village fell into ruin.

But a bunch of enthusiastic Welsh people saw a chance to revive the village and revive Welsh at the same time. Funds were raised, and it was bought to create a centre for learning Welsh. Today it is a vibrant place again and still retains its former histories.

On the 'Miga-moga'

Down the Miga-moga, through the mist,
Past Cwt y Gwyddal, outcrops and rushes.

Cliffs to westward, screech of bird-king,
To the east the flames are burning.

On the Miga-moga Beuno's bell rings
'Come to the fountain, here is cleansing'.

Stone by stone monks raised a house up high,
Their hollow eyes lifting like red kites.

Up the Miga-moga all is grey and raw,
Till the fishermen bring nets ashore.

Seasons of farming, strong sun overhead;
Myths in the depths of the wood.

Down the Miga-moga a name called out,
Clynnog Fawr's empty but spirits are about.

Fields are neglected one by one:
Cae Cefn Sgubor, Cae Tan yr Hendy, Cae Pin.

On the Miga-moga, heavy boots of afternoon,
Workers chiselling at rock, a craft rewarding.

Leaving Porth y Nant, last quarry steamer,
Wicklow's hills beckon, another future.

Up the Miga-moga, someone with a dream,
Seeking new life where ruins have been.

See the dream not long becoming
Houses where the language is growing.

A zig-zag road, a reality,
At the Miga-moga, between rocks and sea.

The Miners' Strike

Traditionally, Welsh miners were well known for insisting on their rights from the mine owners. The work was dangerous and there is a long record of disasters in the Welsh industry. Thousands of miners suffered from serious injuries and were incapacitated by the effects of underground dust.

The miners argued for better pay because of facing such danger, and also insisted on compensation for the families of those suffering with industrial diseases and the consequence of accidents. As coal was needed for energy and heating for just about every house and industry, a strike by miners affected the whole country and the miners' unions could even be a threat to national governments.

For their part, because of the industry's importance and the high demand for coal, the government was often ready to use violence to break miners' strikes. South Wales miners faced soldiers and armed police on more than one occasion.

In 1984, Margaret Thatcher's government announced its intention to 'modernise' the British coal mining industry. This meant closing a great many mines and throwing thousands of miners out of work. The miners fought for a place at the table to negotiate the future of their industry, as it was they who knew and understood it. The National Union of Mineworkers and the government reached deadlock. A strike ensued from March 1984 to March 1985, lasting over a year. During that time there were many bloody skirmishes between picketing miners and the ranks of police sent to contain them.

On the whole the Welsh miners upheld the strike. This was a strike for work and a future for the villages and valleys: a strike to save communities. Their wives, mothers and daughters supported the strikers, and throughout Wales money was raised and food collected for striking families.

It grew to become a national battle here in Wales – about the nation's right to run its own economy rather than having to swallow harsh decisions taken in Westminster. Many believe that one of the results of the Miners' Strike was that Wales voted to have its own Assembly in 1997.

In March 1985 the miners returned to work, having won nothing. The Coal Board closed dozens of mines in Wales and 20,000 miners lost their jobs in the years that followed. There was dire unemployment and poverty in the valleys that had once seen the zenith of the industry.

But back went the miners on 7 March 1985, behind their brass bands and colourful banners. The words on one banner read 'This is the end. The end of the beginning.' The politician Adam Price was sixteen at the time. His father was part of the strike at the Betws colliery in the Amman Valley. The lad was inspired by the strikers' energy and determination, sticking to their campaign for a better future for all of Wales.

Events at the last deep mine in Wales – Tower Colliery in Hirwaun – illustrate this new determination. 'British Coal', the owners of the mine, closed Tower Colliery in 1994, arguing that is was uneconomic. The 239 miners each used their £8,000 redundancy payment to buy the colliery for £2 million. The mine re-opened in January 1995 and was the largest employer in the area until the coal ran out in 2008. The story remains a testament to the miners' vision: they saw that it was time for us to run our country's economy ourselves.

An end, yet a beginning

This is the end
Yet a new beginning,
A different order
To our dates and days;
The end of sharing
Amongst ourselves,
Yet the first steps
Towards our freedom.

This is the end
Of Pwll y Betws,
But men are emerging
Out of their cages;
Tomorrow no more
Country of the Workhouse,
Our children will seek
Other answers and places.

This is the end
Of the thrashing of workers,
There's a light
At the top of Tower;
End of being governed,
Beginning of a climb
Like a newly-married husband.

This is the end
Of a coalfield colony,
Of those grave galleries;
Beginning of a long walk
To become free.

A Stadium for the New Millennium

Rugby is a national sport in Wales: its red-shirted team has achieved amazing feats in the past. In 1999 a new stadium opened beside the Taff, in the heart of Cardiff, and is widely regarded as one of the best grounds in the world. It is rare to have a 74,500-seater stadium in the middle of a busy capital city and, of course, the atmosphere is fantastic, especially when the roof is closed.

Since the stadium's opening, the place and the supporters have inspired the Welsh national team to memorable victories. These include beating South Africa for the first time ever (1999); three Grand Slams (2005, 2008, 2012); European champions (2013) and several unforgettable tries by exciting players such as Shane Williams, George North and Jamie Roberts.

Wales 30–3 England

(Millennium Stadium, Cardiff, 2013)

'Land of My Fathers' rose up like steam,
Cheering to the roof first kick of the game,
Red dragon flags, their wings beating,
From every valley the people singing.

The English team with jerseys of white
Unable to cope, losing the fight;
Their fans thought they'd own the afternoon,
Both Championship and Triple Crown.

Their forwards so tough and backs so strong –
Ready for tries, sure of celebration;
And Wales needed equally to win
To become champions of the Six Nations.

Every scrum saw Adam a mini-mountain,
Every ball caught from the air so clean,
Every line-out, the backs running free,
Every kick a success for Halfpenny.

Action unfolded, crowds voices lifted,
England's plans like lovers' jilted,
Every aspect of the game Wales won:
Half time 9-3 … and more to come!

It was a record-breaking second half,
Quick as a hawk moving fifty yards
Skilfully handled and rapidly running
Cuthbert twice crossed the line.

'Land of My Fathers' had finally won,
Red on the Cup at the end of the game,
The English defeated, a record victory,
In the stadium named for a new century.

Our Own Assembly

In 1997, almost six hundred years after Owain Glyndŵr held his parliaments, Wales voted for powers to govern itself. The Assembly is housed in Cardiff Bay, and its new building opened in 2006. A large majority voted in 2011 to give the Assembly more power.

This was an important milestone on the long journey of the people of Wales to establish a fully accomplished country of their own. We have the National Library, a National Museum, universities, a disestablished church, independent chapels, a capital city, a National Opera, and two National Theatres. Arguably more important than any of these, is that Welsh has once again been reinstated as an official language in Wales. The long-held dream of Glyndŵr is being realised.

During the twenty-first century our country will build on all of this, take more and more responsibility for its own affairs and adopt an independent voice in the world community. The large countries have created enough of a mess in the twentieth century – maybe this one will be the century of the small countries.

Among the laws passed in the early years of the new Assembly were ones to award compensation to quarrymen's widows, limit plastic bags, ban smoking in public buildings, strengthen the Welsh language, and make organ donation easier.

It pays to look back at our history, to

remember the twists and turns in the journey, and
to stride ahead confidently to the future.

A new country

'We see a new country,' say the young,
'One which honours Glyndŵr,
Where the lark is rising
And no valleys drowned by water.

'See a new country without walls
To keep us in division,
Country not bowing to Caesar,
Memories of righteous indignation.

'See a new country without the dust
Infecting the air and lungs,
Without a fear of prison
When the wrong words are on tongues.

'See a new country, no gates and tolls
Halting those upon their way,
With a future embraced by all
And true respect for history.

'See a new country,' say the young,
'Sculpted by our hands:
Fingers shaping its destiny,
From coal and slate a building stands.'

Part of History

The stories that make up the history of Wales are not 'once upon a time' stories – they are part of our own story, and the story of children in Wales in the future. When we hear of the Celts and the Brythons; of Arthur's knights and Owain Glyndŵr's soldiers; Merched Beca and the children forced to bear the Welsh Not, we must remember that they are all part of us. As we hear our history – be it through story, verse or song – we feel as they did. That is how we know where we have come from, and which path to choose to take us forward into the future.

Legendary children's author T. Llew Jones was a wizard with words, able to get his readers to 'feel' his stories. The centenary of his birth was celebrated in 2015. I was besotted with his books as a boy; I still enjoy them and still feel the thrill of stepping into the shoes of the characters. Through the talent of storytellers like T. Llew Jones, generations of children from Wales have felt part of the country's history.

Being part of Welsh history

I'm on a dangerous road
Far from the warmth of home,
There are men wearing cloaks
And nightmarish horses roam;
Scurrilous thieves are following,
Bare-knuckle fighters and cattlemen,
The moon is a warning.

I hear the cry of the captain
As all the sails are set,
The treasure of the pirates
Somewhere beyond the horizon;
I see a grin broaden
On the face of Harri Morgan,
His scars from Spanish swordsmen.

I'm standing with the bandits
With bow at the ready,
To take revenge on the Baron
Who's treated us so badly;
All young brothers tonight
With blood on their hands,
Toppling that Baron's might.